Down the length of Africa, from the Red Sea to the Kalahari Desert, lies a series of waterways, like a gleaming string of pearls. Strung together along the East African Rift Valley, the Nile River, Lake Turkana, Lake Kyoga, Lake Victoria, Lake Tanganyika, Lake Malawi, the Zambezi/Luangwa Valley, the Victoria Falls and, lastly, the Okavango Delta provide surface evidence of the many geological forces that are shaping the continent.

Made up of loose combinations of very large chunks of material known as cratons, the various continents are less dense and more brittle in substance than the remaining 99,9 per cent of the earth. The earth's crust, consisting of ocean beds and surface landforms, bears the same proportional size to its inner core and mantle as does the skin of an orange to its pith and pulp. Currents in the flexible mantle are constantly moving and rearranging cratons, and just as over the millennia the old land masses have been broken up to form the continents of today, Africa is slowly but surely being torn apart along what is known as the East African Rift System.

The process of rifting exploits the weak links between cratons, shifting the huge blocks apart along faultlines. Material inside the rift zone walls subsides into these gaps to form a graben, or rift valley. A careful examination of the distribution of Africa's earthquakes — good signals of faulting — reveals a bifurcation of the rift just south of Lake Tanganyika. The Lake Malawi branch of this split branches yet again, and these branches meet again, finally, in northern Botswana, to form the Okavango Delta — the last pearl.

Currently active owing to rift propagation and the weight of sediment on the graben floor, the Delta's bounding faults are manifest in a series of micro-earthquakes — on average one 'event' every two days. Satellite images provide striking illustrations of the major graben faults running parallel, north-east to south-west, across the upper and lower parts of the Delta, met perpendicularly by the Panhandle fault zone, which continues down the south-western side of Chief's Island. The Gomare-Kunyere-Thamalakane graben is criss-crossed by minor 'parasitic' faults, which generate slight, progressive gradient changes, though the effect is always lessened by a blanket of sand hundreds of metres thick. The Okavango River, running between the Panhandle faults, crosses the Gomare faultline and spreads sediment outwards in major distributary channels, large lagoon systems and later broad, seasonally flooded plains and increasingly smaller channels — the Okavango swamps.

Although faulting may shape the general morphology of the Delta (known to geomorphologists as an alluvial fan), it is the fine balance between water, plant, sand and animal that determines what will be island and floodplain, where the channels will flow, and for what duration.

The Swamp Book

Perspective
and
Description
of the
Natural Elements
and
Resources
of the
Okavango Delta

Photographs
BOB FORRESTER
Text
MIKE MURRAY-HUDSON
Design
LANCE CHERRY

SOUTHERN
BOOK PUBLISHERS

Text copyright © 1989 by M. Murray-Hudson
Photography copyright © 1989 by B. Forrester

ISBN 1 86812 154 2

First edition, first impression 1989

Published by, Southern Book Publishers (Pty) Ltd,
PO Box 548, Bergvlei 2012, Johannesburg

Cover design by Michael Barnett

Reproduction and setting by Unifoto, Cape Town
Set in 10 on 11 pt. Megaron Light

Printed on 135 gsm Shaka gloss

Printed and bound by
National Book Printers, Cape Town

Water lilies (Nymphaea capensis) take advantage of still or slow-moving water.

Hydrocynus forskalii . . . 'water dog'.

African fish eagle (Haliaeetus vocifer) swoops and kills.

Pygmy goose (Nettapus auritus). Doyen of the floodplains.

Annually the water recedes, leaving dry grassy plains.

Lily trotter (Actophilornus africanus) by name and nature.

Contents

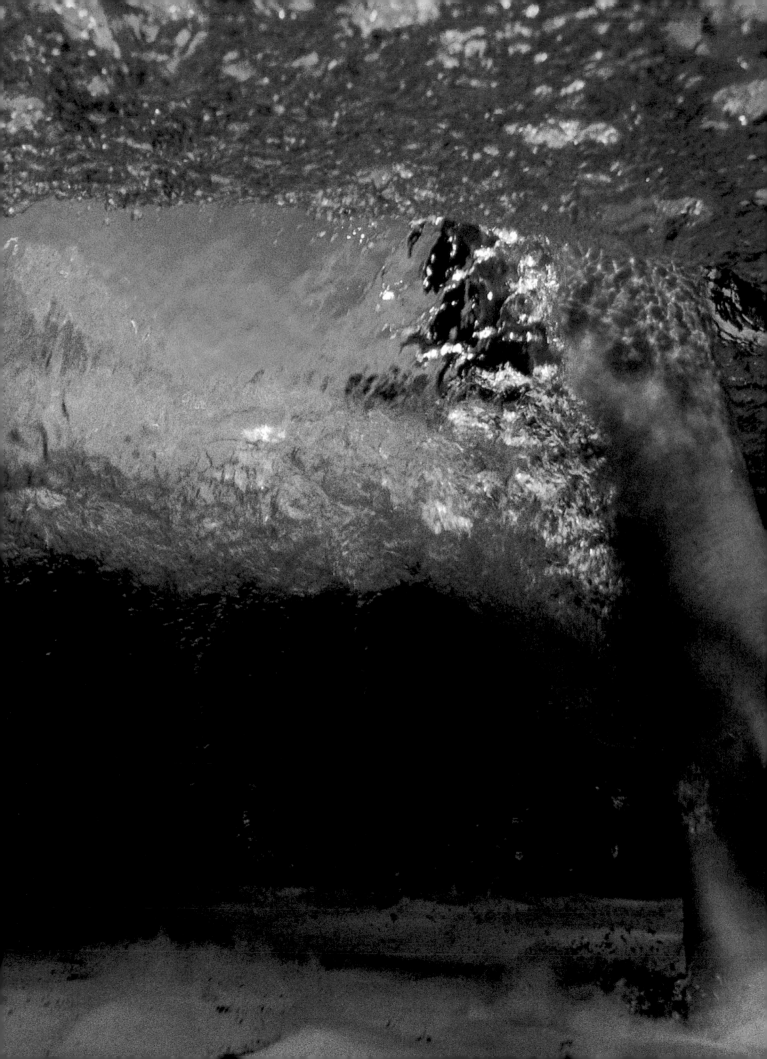

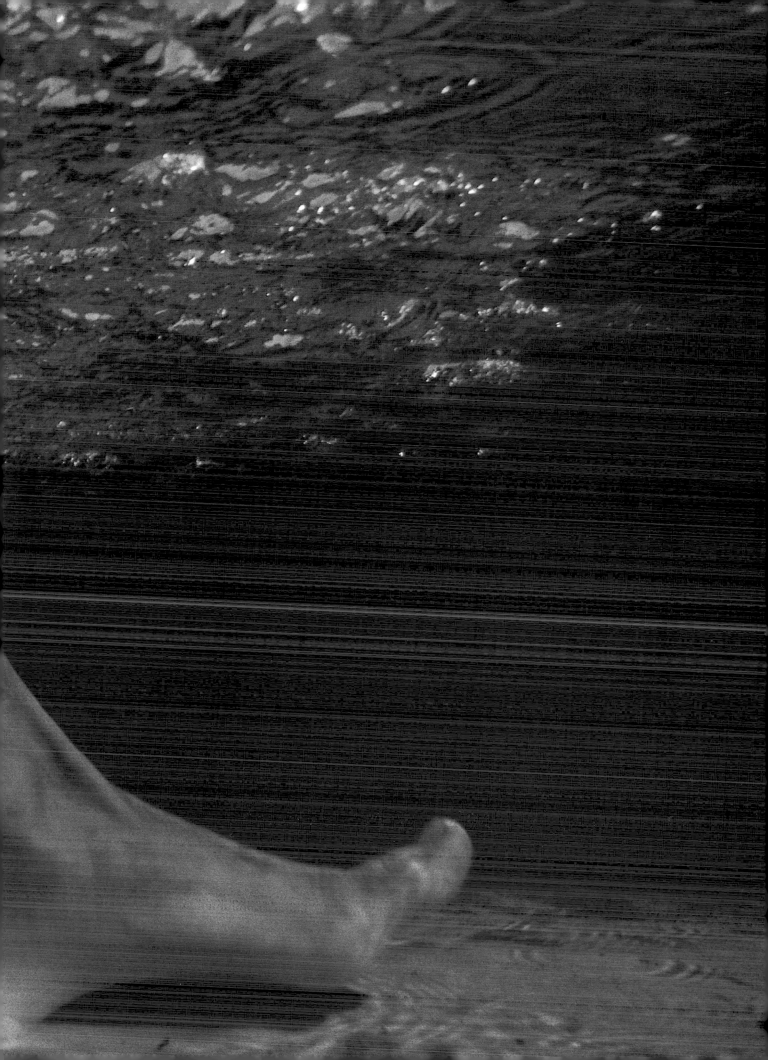

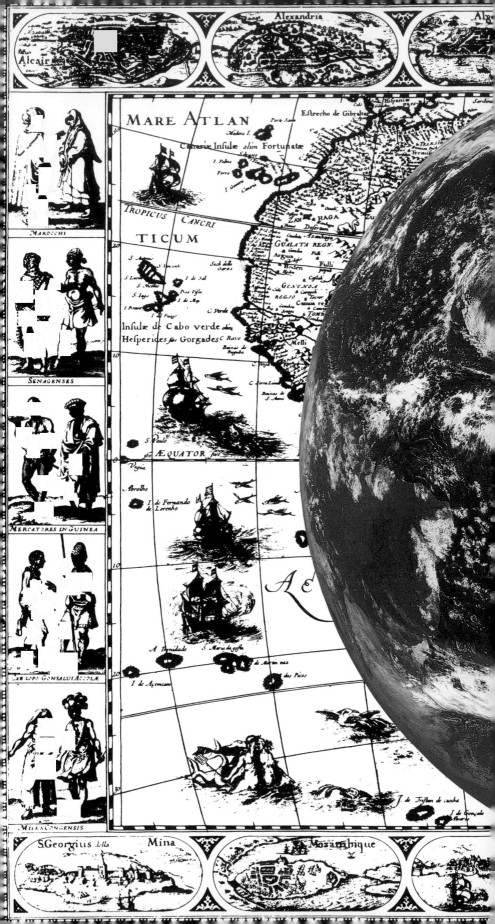

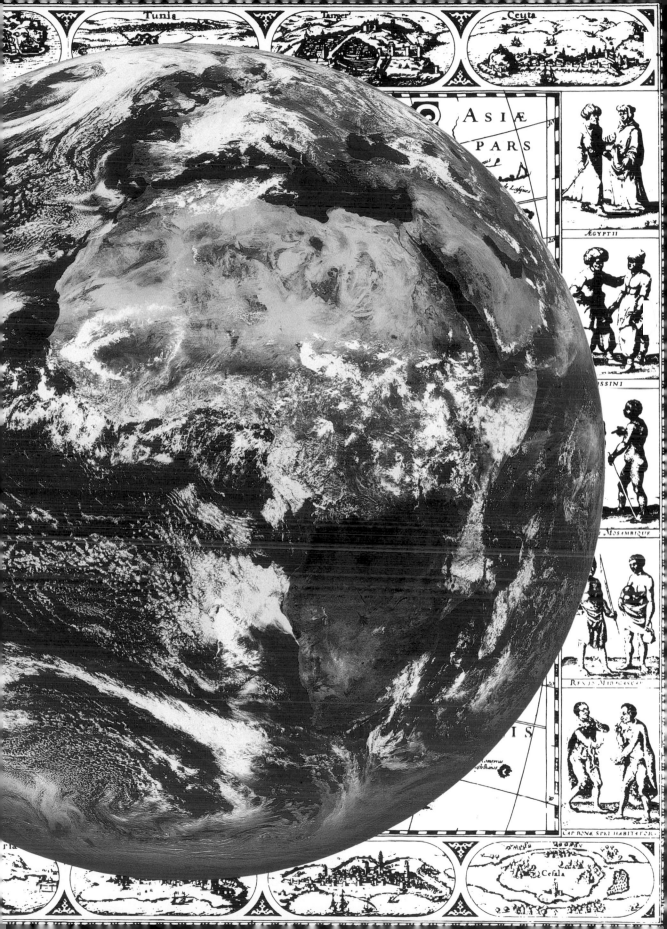

ASIÆ

PARS

Tunis

Tanger

Ceuta

ÆGYPTII

MOSAMBIQUE

REX IS MADAGASCAR

CAP BONÆ SPEI HABITATOR

Cefala

Reminiscences of the colonial era

"In 1911 my father said to me: 'My son, we cannot stay here in Windhoek. There is going to be a war and we will be prisoners. I know of a place called Ngamiland.' "

MARTIN THOMAS KAYES, MAUN RESIDENT, 1988

'On every side as far as the eye could see, lay stretched a sea of fresh water, in many places concealed from sight by a covering of reeds and rushes of every shade and hue; whilst numerous islands, spread over its whole surface, and adorned with rich vegetation, gave to the whole an indescribably beautiful appearance."

CHARLES ANDERSSON, EXPLORER, 1856

The path from Seronga to Gabamukuni skirted the northern edge of the swamps, leaving the Okavango behind and going eastward. It was a very hot day in November 1953 and we had tried to obtain horses or donkeys for the trip but no one would risk them to the tsetse fly, so we had to walk. My job then was to revise the tax registers throughout Ngamiland, so we had driven from the D.C's office in Maun along the Thamalakane to Toteng, via Sehithwa and Tsau to Nokaneng (where we spent the night at Andrew Wright's trading store) and on to Sepopa the next day. We crossed the Okavango to Seronga in mekoro (sing. mokoro) (dug-outs) and camped there near the village before setting out early next morning for Gabamukuni.

Some two months since I had left Southampton in the *Winchester Castle* for Cape Town. From there I had travelled via Mafikeng and Francistown by train and truck to Maun, where I had been posted as a District Officer Cadet.

Crocodiles (Crocodilus niloticus) **prey on creatures of the air, land and water.**

Because the footpath was close to the Delta we had to wade through knee-deep molapos (flood channels) and then climb sandy ridges to the next molapo, and so on. The water was clear and beautifully cool, but the leeches were less delightful. Our party consisted of our driver, who was an excellent linguist and shot, the District Messenger, a young Police Constable, the Chief's Representative from Seronga and a young boy acompanying him. I carried a rifle, given to me by an uncle who had used it on Indian bears. It seemed to get heavier at every step.

I was told that no European had been to Gabamukuni for many years. Certainly I had the impression that had I made the trip 20 or even perhaps 50 years earlier, there would have been little difference in the surrounding country or even in the habits and possessions of the people. In fact we saw almost no-one on the path, but plenty of game and tsetse. Nor were there any domestic animals at all until we reached Gabamukuni, where some of the people owned goats. The people lived by fishing, hunting game and growing sorghum, beans, melons, pumpkins and such in the molapo as the annual floods receded. East of Seronga and on toward the Caprivi in the north-east there were no signs at all of the Protectorate Government. No police posts, schools, dispensaries, roads, post offices, trading stores and very few people. Remoteness and the tsetse fly had, up till then, ensured that little human impact had been made on the area since the Bayei migrations of 1750. There were, of course, guns (often muzzle loaders), metal hoes, knives and pots, but very few other signs of outside influence. A bicycle was an extreme rarity because of its cost and the ever-present thick cover of white sand through which it was almost impossible to ride.

As we waded through one molapo we saw a herd of impala on the far bank. Although I had had some small success shooting crocodiles, I had not yet had a chance at a buck. Everyone was waiting to see how the new young Molaodi would make out. It seemed to me that the foresight of my gun wavered in a constant circle of some two inches! However, there were so many impala that it was not too easy to miss. I fired and saw one fall over, then heard a shot from the expert, Jack Ramsden. We discovered that my bullet had gone through both hocks! Jack's, of course, went straight into the heart. I never became a good shot, nor did I really enjoy it, and after a year or so confined myself to birds.

When, after an exhausting march, we arrived at Gabamukuni we were royally welcomed by the inhabitants, despite the unpopularity of our tax register mission. In fact one of the more enthusiastic villagers composed a song about us, on the spot, which went something like

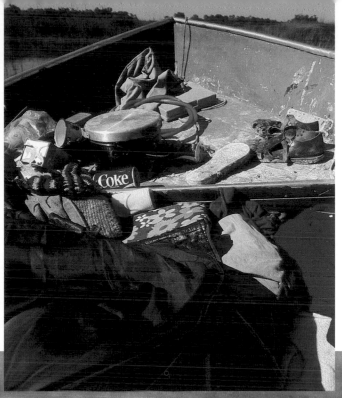

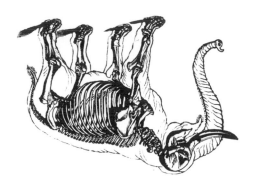

Dragonflies (Brachythemis sp) add a rare hue to the green-brown landscape.

Paraphernalia for a short excursion.

The African hippopotamus (Hippopotamus amphibius) takes its toll of humans in the Okavango every year.

Lekgowa le lekgowa Gabamukuni mua!
Moherero le moherero Gabamukuni mua!
Motawana le Motawana Gabamukuni mua!

and so on. This, it was explained, meant "A European has come to Gabamukuni, a Herero has come to Gabamukuni, a Motawana has come to Gabamukuni"! All strangers.

That evening we cooked the impala and most of a kudu — shot again by Jack — and a lot of meat was consumed by a lot of people. Despite a steady drizzle of rain we slept quite well under some big trees until morning. It took most of the next day to update the tax register particulars relating to the area and after a further night, dry this time, we set off back to Seronga.

If anything the sun seemed even more scorching on the way back and every now and again I stopped to turn round, simply to shade the exposed side of my body for a bit of relief.

Toward sunset we arrived back in Seronga and the next morning boarded our mekoro again for the cross-river trip to Sepopa, where we had left our truck to drive back to Maun. In those days, the roads were two deep tracks in the fine white sand that covers the Delta area. In places of very heavy sand the road was corrugated with

The subadult waterbuck (Kobus ellipsiprymnus) *will eventually reach 1,7 metres at the shoulder.*

Stiletto paradigm. Long, splayed toes spread the jacana's weight.

mopane poles, which caused the vehicles to shudder and shake as though traversing an endless and badly made grid. One scarcely saw another truck on the road. Occasionally one would pass a WNLA (mine labour recruiters) truck or a trader's vehicle carrying goods for the few stores outside Maun, at Sehithwa, Tsau, Nokaneng and Shakawe. Bridges across the Thamalakane or the Thaoge were made of large mopane poles and had to be negotiated carefully and repaired frequently. There were, of course, no garages outside Maun itself and one was dependent upon the skill and ingenuity of one's co-travellers, which was often of a very high standard.

The mid-1950s were years of about average rainfall and rivers and molapos were full and vegetation abundant. Travelling the Shakawe – Sehithwa road one passed large herds of buffalo, wildebeest, impala and zebra and often saw elephant. Further west, away from the open water, were herds of gemsbok. There was virtually no hunting for sport and hardly any sporting visitors. Near the outskirts of Sehithwa we met a small band of Herero horsemen.

Cool relief from 41 degree Celsius summer sun.

Vegetation in the seasonal swamp feeds and hides myriad fish.

The tourist and the swamper. A question of style and values.

Squacco heron (Ardeola ralloides) in flight.

Huge flocks of greater flamingos (Phoenicopterus ruber) thrive in the evaporating shallows of Lake Ngami, one of the outflows of the Delta. The saline remnants in the water sustain the brine shrimp, which keeps the birds both fed and pink. Flamingos are genetically white, their pigmentation developing from their diet. American zoos place pink dye in their food. Small filters inside their beaks help the birds feed with their heads upside down.

Aerial reflections.

Still surface.

Oxygen weed (Lagarosiphon major) *.*

Satellite image. In the Kalahari Desert the Okavango River strikes a shallow gradient and spreads itself into a fan shape. Most of the water is lost through evaporation and a meagre live per cent reaches the Delta's southern limits.

Wet winds and rolling dunes

Geomorphology

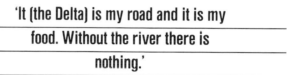

Linyanti-Chobe drainage
north-eastwards, formin
border. A decline in rain
shallow expanses of the
dehydrate progressively
system's wetlands to sh
18 000 square kilometre

Deltas are characteri
carried into still bodies o
rivers. When a river enc
a gradient decrease, flo
sediment is deposited. A
channels have spread b
million tonnes of sedime
ever-widening triangle.
tonnes of sand would bu
a metre from Paris to At
under a layer half a met

It is only in the chann
flows fast enough to trar
channels may be seen
Delta, carrying the sand
that become progressiv
channels constitute only
Delta's total area, they c
incoming material. The
of a dune on a channel
along the bank, which is
and redeposited elsewh

The sediment distribu
irregular. Channels are
vegetation — most sign
grasses — whose fibrou
sand from leaving the c

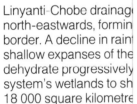

Nearly one and a half metres of annual summer rainfall is collected and filtered by the eastern vegetated slopes of the central Angolan highlands, the 'Planalto Central'. Springs from peaty sponges join to form the crystal-clear, fast-flowing upper reaches of the Cubango River, which runs through a series of rocky rapids before dropping more than 500 metres to turn eastwards and meet the Cuito, a sister river from the same catchment area. Gentler gradients after the junction permit the first development of swampy vegetation, which increases as the combined currents flow into the meandering Okavango River. The seasonal rainfall generates a wave of water from Angola, over the Popa Falls

in Namibia's thin Caprivi Strip, and into Botswana, where it sweeps down the Okavango River and more sedately into the Delta triangle. Low gradients and dense vegetation temper the flow, forcing it to fill extensive floodplains and saturate sandy soils before finally allowing the remainder to dribble into Lake Ngami and the Makgadikgadi Pans.

A satellite image revealing the geology of the

The last bend before home.

Meandering curves in the dry season _inside bends, and bed load sand roll_ _undulating dunes._

Tention due to incipient rifting. Previ _Makgadikgadi pans._

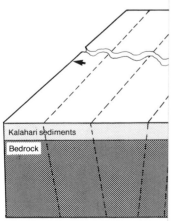

Kalahari sediments

Bedrock

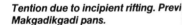

Fractures representing incipient f

banks in the Delta to aggrade rather than erode. The sand is trapped on the channel bed, where sediment added annually causes the bed level to rise. Vegetated banks grow at the same rate, by filtering the flood waters seeping out over the levees into the floodplains, and permitting only suspended organic detritus, fine silt and clays to pass. Slow-flowing water in the floodplains ensures that these substances settle and accumulate, ultimately to form peat-like, largely organic, matter.

The aggradation of the channel is a continuous process. Decreasing gradients and consequently increasing sedimentation and encroaching fringe vegetation contribute to an insidious, slow blocking of the channel. These constrictions provide easy lodging for drifting flotsam that adds to the congestion, and the blockages are made even more dense by invading rhizomatous plants. The growing difference in elevation between channel and floodplain eventually forces the water and its sediment load in the upper reaches of the channel into an alternative course.

A breach in the outside bend of a meander, an extra high flood level, a wandering hippo breaching a weak levee, or a tuft of vegetation on a channel bank diverting new flood water, may all allow the current to follow the increased gradient from main channel to floodplain. This change in direction is ever in evidence. A tree grows on a low-lying floodplain island and is burnt flush to the ground by seasonal fires. The displaced flood water covers the roots, eroding the sand around it until it is held only by a deep tap root, which eventually rots and disintegrates, adding new nutrients to the system. A climatic factor like a poor rain season in Angola means a relatively small flood and low flow velocity that in turn also assists the dynamic vegetative and relief forces in changing the direction of the channel.

While a riverine ecology is being generated along the newly forming watercourse, the previous channel and floodplains are abandoned and may dry up. Decay of organic sediments causes the floodplains to sink in places (sometimes accelerated by underground peat fires), further accentuating the relief differences between the raised channel sands and old floodplains.

Termites (_Macrotermes_ sp), yet another factor shaping the Delta's morphology, use the inorganic floodplain residues, the fine clay deposits, for termitaria construction. Dry floodplains are rapidly colonised and spires built to enable termite colonies to survive possible inundation. Eventual reflooding of the area leaves a topography common to the middle and upper Delta: long, sandy island chains (relics of the abandoned, raised channels) are surrounded by floodplains dotted with termite mounds,

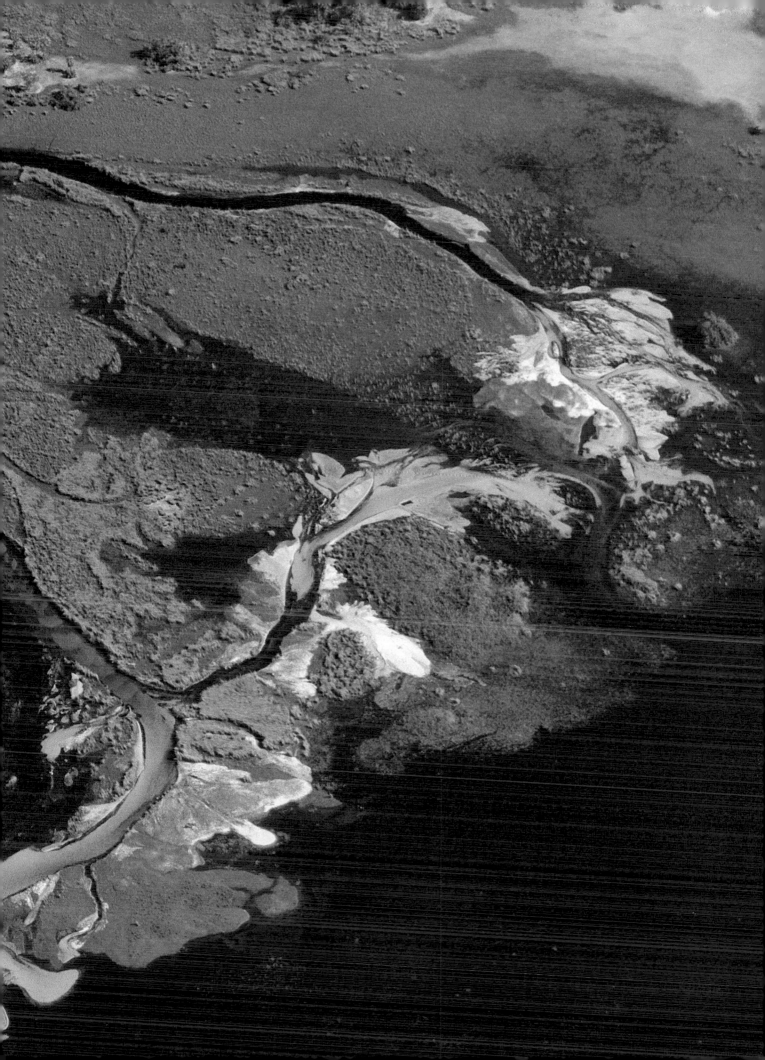

Terrapin (Pelomedusa sp), tiny fat mouse (Steatomys pratensis), bushbuck (Tragelaphus scriptus), tree squirrel (Paraxerus arundinum)

themselves ultimately forming small, densely vegetated islands.

While channels form the transport system of the Delta, it is the floodplains that accommodate the bulk of the flowing water. Up to 1 000 tonnes of water per second may flow down the Okavango River at the peak of a high flood. The gentler channel gradients below the Gomare faultline are incapable of coping with this enormous volume. Most of the water seeps slowly through the heavily vegetated floodplains, bearing fresh nutrients to hungry aquatic plants in the upper Delta, and sustenance to dry grasses and sedges in the lower sections of the swamp.

The seasonal swamp, where large shallow plains are annually flooded and then flushed dry, has the dynamics to sustain a large variety of plant and animal life. The permanent water areas in the northern part of the fan-shaped Delta do not have as much constantly changing vegetation or so many feeding grounds, and support a far smaller variety of flora and fauna. But in nature there are always relationships of dependency: one section of the swamp supports the other. The permanent core of water joins the input of the Panhandle to the seasonal extremities of the Delta area. Were this core to diminish along with the volume of the Panhandle's input, so too would the outer reaches, and subsequently the great variety of plant and animal life that the Delta is presently capable of sustaining.

Delta within a delta. In the permanent swamp a channel encounters a gradient decrease and is forced to spread outwards across previous sedimentation.

"Moswaoeme" . . . He is dead but still standing. Camel-thorn tree root (Acacia erioloba) after seasonal fires and the change of a channel's path.

African hippopotamus
(Hippopotamus amphibius)

With only two bulbous eyes visible some 50 centimetres apart above the water, joined by the gentle curve of a dark grey forehead, you may never know the hippo is there, but for a slight movement, perhaps of an ear tip. Responsible for more human deaths than any other mammal in Africa, the hippopotamus has the size, agility, temperament, teeth and legend to demand the respect it deserves in and around the waterways of the swamp. Local mourning processions bear witness to the ferocity of an animal which need fear no predator, yet which will defend its territory more belligerently and vigorously than most creatures. The narrow channels of the swamp leave little room for evasion of these two-tonne beasts. Confronted with a mokoro or canoe big enough to pose a potential threat, the hippo will either quietly submerge and act as innocuously as possible, or, more often than not, surge through the water with devastating speed, jaws agape, and crunch viciously down on its target.

Left alone, however, they seem the most placid of giants, lying in the mud and on sand banks, allowing the water to flow gently over their backs to prevent the sun from drying and splitting their skins. Hippos with cracked hides can be seen in certain areas in the low-water season when glistening red oil is secreted by the skin to moisten the mud-hardened cracks.

Hippos are herbivorous, nocturnal feeders, and towards sunset, as the air cools down, they begin to roam from island to island in search of their favourite grasses. Woe betide the person who crosses their path at this time! Out of the water, hippos are very vulnerable to hunters and poachers and should they take fright while feeding, will head straight back to their swampy sanctuary. Anybody in the way will be summarily trampled upon.

Sociable 'Delta hippo' generally live in small herds, though they are found singly or in pairs in the narrower streams. Their aggression is also displayed in battles for group supremacy and dominance in mating. The hippo is one of the few mammals that will fight to the death, and their bloody battles often leave the loser dying from horrifying wounds. Apart from man, parasites are the only creatures capable of killing adult hippos.

Hippos mark their territory with their faeces, and by vigorously wagging their short tails they may spread their excrement several metres up tree trunks, marking specific islands as the grazing territory of an individual or herd.

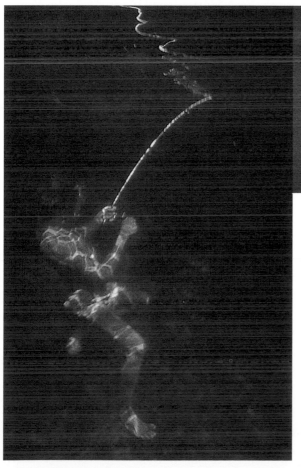

A wild date palm (Phoenix reclinata) *leans out in characteristic form from a small Panhandle island. Papyrus lines the far bank.*

Reed cormorant (Phalacrocorax africanus) *drying its wings.*

Submerged angler catching supper.

The tiger fish is a fine sporting species, leaping spectacularly when hooked.

A solitary old red sand dune, 'Redcliffs', formed when the Kalahari was drier, rises above the Panhandle.

Terrapin oblivious to photographer nearby with flashing camera.

A bound papyrus raft (huzhenje) stabilised by mekoro carries thatching grass down the Panhandle. In the past the rafts were used extensively for hippo hunting because they were safer than mekoro.

Little egret (Egretta garzetta) in classical wader pose.

A shy sitatunga doe (Tragelaphus spekei) *browses in wet grasslands on the edge of a permanent swamp island.*

Paddling a disabled motor boat for miles is no joke.

Lily pads from a fish eye view.

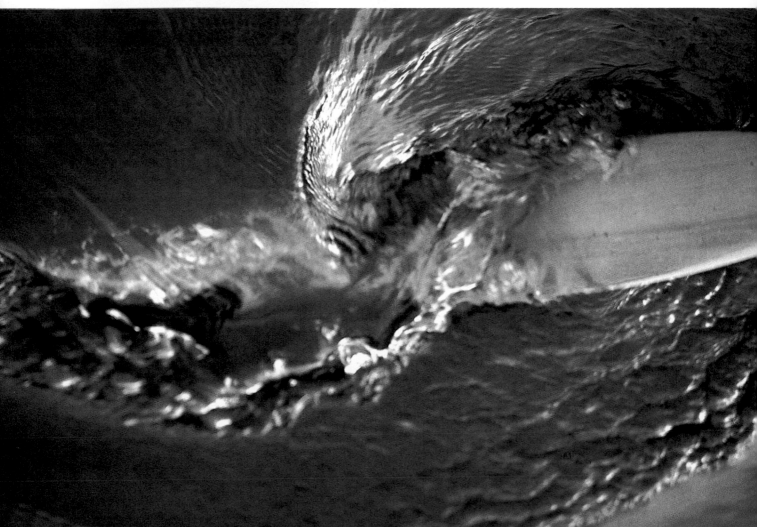

The Okavango River is as wide as 250 metres near Mohembo, on Botswana's northern border.

Darters, whitebreasted and reed cormorants, and squacco herons (*Anhinga melanogaster, Phalacrocorax carbo, P. africanus, Ardeola ralloides*) use the thickets for nesting and breeding. Here the birds are safe from landbased predators, and most aquatic predators are unable to reach their nests of twigs and grass.

The wild date palm (*Phoenix reclinata*), is often found drooping over the passing flow, and offers excellent perches to raptors seeking local bream like the Mozambique and greenhead tilapia (*Oreochromus mossambicus, O. macrochir*) and the prized tiger fish (*Hydrocynus forskhalii*), an angling favourite.

Sharp-toothed and blunt-toothed catfish (*Clarias gariepinus, C. ngamensis*) are very conspicuous during the early summer months in what is known as the 'barbel runs'. As the water recedes, small fish — bulldogs and churchills (*Marcusenius macrolepidotus, Petrocephalus catostoma*) — leaving the floodplains seek shelter in the papyrus-rimmed channel fringes. Packs of catfish patrol the river's edges as they move slowly upstream in search of permanent backwaters, and gorge themselves on the fleeing fish. It is thought that catfish prey predominantly on mormyrids because they are able to detect small electrical impulses emitted by the latter. Large packs of tiger fish also abound, tearing large chunks out of the catfish and preying on the mormyrids, while crocodiles (*Crocodilus niloticus*) eat their share of catfish as well. Flocks of birds (cormorants, darters, kingfishers, herons, storks and eagles) may be seen wheeling above, scooping up pieces of flesh floating to the surface. Largemouthed bream like the thinface largemouth and nembwe (*Serranochromis angusticeps, S. robustus jallae*) join in the scavenging.

Flocks of gregarious whitefronted bee-eaters (*Merops bullockoides*) nest in the vertical sides of the eroded banks. Their communal living habits seem to stem from neither a safety instinct nor breeding or food-gathering strategies, but from a lack of suitable nesting sites along the main channel. Their burrows, often forged a metre

inwards, greatly reduce access to predators such as snakes, monitor lizards and raptors.

Subtly marked insects and frogs buzz along the river's edge and into the floodplains. Perennially inundated with water, though sometimes cut off from the main channel by levees in the drier season, these floodplains are mostly inhospitable to the larger mammals. Thick, frequently razorsharp or serrated sedges and aquatic grasses (*Scirpus cubensis, Miscanthus junceus, Vetiveria* sp) generally offer access only to the shy, swamp-adapted sitatunga antelope (*Tragelaphus spekei*) and hippopotamus. Fire, nature's scourge in dry climates, regularly destroys the foliage right down to the water's edge. Flocks of birds are then attracted by small water animals and previously unexposed water flora (water lily seeds, sedge seeds and corms).

Nowhere else in the Delta are contrasts in vegetation as noticeable as further down the Panhandle. The meandering boundary between the floodplain and the desert-banked trough-edge puts arid and swamp flora and fauna in a strange juxtaposition. The sandy desert is a land of guinea-fowl (*Numida meleagris*), silver-leaf terminalia trees (*Terminalia sericea*), the crimsonbreasted shrike (*Laniarius atrococcineus*) and the purple, yellow and white-flowered sickle bush (*Dichrostachys cinerea*), which is a primary invader of overgrazed areas and whose spiky branches slash vehicle tyres to pieces. In the scorching hot, orange-coloured dunes you may even surprise a crocodile basking in the sun, and it is wise to remember that crocodiles are exceedingly fast on dry land.

The harsh desert landscape often ends abruptly at the river and floodplain border of lush green papyrus, grasses (*Vossia cuspidata*), sedges and trees (*Diospyros* sp, *Garcinia* sp) inhabited by twittering kingfishers, fish eagles and hippo.

Hippo will fight to the death if neither side retreats. The battle is fierce and bloody and the bulls often leave huge gashes in each other in their struggle for supremacy.

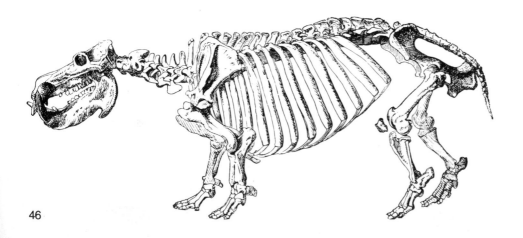

African fish eagle
(Haliaeetus vocifer)

In the uppermost reaches of a riverside tree, with the gleaming white V of its chest emblazoned against the dark brown and black of the rest of its body, perches the African fish eagle — king of the swamp skies. With its two-metre wingspan and aerodynamically upturned wingtips, it is able to rise and glide effortlessly from thermal to thermal.

The expression 'eagle-eyed' is founded on fact. The fish eagle is able to see clearly eight times as far as man, with a vast range of vision. They can spot their prey from kilometres up and will plummet with lightning speed to snatch a fish out of the water, a snake off the surface of the water, or a cormorant chick still confined to its nest.

The most common of the local birds of prey, the African fish eagle is also the most territorial. The waters of the swamp are clearly divided into distinct territories dominated by either one or a pair of fish eagles. These areas grow larger or smaller as the flood waters rise and recede. Presiding over a territory is the only guarantee for survival, and this right must be fought for, with the ferocity of talons and beaks the deciding factor. Juvenile fish eagles, if they survive the dangers of nest life — snakes and aerial predators — must drive off a resident bird in order to move into a territory. If they fail, they will probably starve to death — the fate of 90 per cent of all young fish eagles in this area. Bedraggled-looking birds can often be seen flying from one territory to the next in their search for an area to occupy.
an area to occupy.

As one moves northwards through the swamps, from the seasonal to the permanent and Panhandle sections, the number of islands and thus viable perches decreases accordingly, as does the number of shallow-water fish. There are in turn, too, fewer fish eagles, each in charge of a hunting territory considerably larger than those further south.

Crocodiles indulge in foreplay.

Chacma baboon (Papio ursinus) 'hanging out'.

Between the broad and the narrow

The permanent swamp

'I am wary of the night. The hippos sound like drums. When the palm leaves "whistle" between the drums, sometimes I forget where I am, and go looking for people.'

XEKANEMA TANIKWA, INNER-SWAMP BUSHMAN DWELLER, b. 1920s

'On a canoe voyage hence to Linyanti, the craft, though moving near the shore, was assaulted by an immense hippopotamus, which shoved against the boat, using its head for the purpose, with such a strength that it was almost lifted out of the water. Fortunately no harm was done to life or limb.'

DAVID CHARLES LIVINGSTONE, EXPLORER, 1855

The Panhandle is like the spout-piece of an inverted funnel. Water gushes into the narrow end, surges down the confining spout, and confronted with a gradient increase, spreads into a 150 degree arc. This arc is the beginning of an incredibly complex system, with slowing currents being forced outwards across ancient sand deposits and gentle rifts.

So the Okavango River proper ends and the swamp begins.

Where the river enters the main Delta graben, it splits into three main distributary channels, the Thaoge River to the west, the Boro River, southwards, and the Nqogha River, eastwards. These three rivers border and bisect the 'permanent' swamp in the northern part of the Delta — the core of the inverted cone.

Cattle egrets (Bubulcus ibis) *bask in the eastern limit of the swamp at Xaxanaxa.*

Tributaries and streams — offshoots of the dominant distributary rivers — dissipate into banks of vegetation and are eventually swallowed by extensive lediba (lagoon) systems. The great volume of water contained in a relatively limited surface area, which deters evaporation, has resulted in a perennially flooded swamp. The maximum and minimum water levels rarely differ by more than 40 or 50 centimetres, unlike the adjacent seasonal swamp where levels may differ by more than two metres. The flood pulse here is not confined by river-beds and levee banks, but also affects both permanently submerged channels and floodplains in a similar fashion.

The circular, semi-circular and elongated islands are structurally similar to those found in the lower Delta, though they seem to be smaller here. In summer, river banks in the seasonal swamp are exposed for basking crocodiles and water monitors, while banks in the permanent swamp remain submerged even when the water volume reaches its ebb. Because of the relatively constant water level, islands do not vary greatly in size from one season to the next. Unlike the dynamic variety of aquatic and dryland flora and fauna dependent on the fluctuations in the seasonal floodplains, populations remain stable in the permanent swamp.

Perennially submerged landforms sustain genuine aquatic plants and water-loving grasses

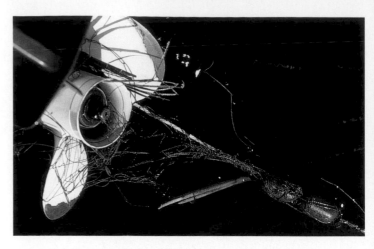

Fish nets strung across the river are difficult to detect.

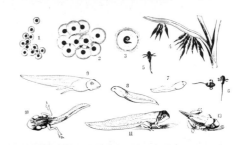

Aquatic plants may be beautiful, but are murderous when they snare a propellor.

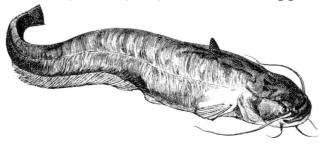

and sedges (*V. cuspidata, Cladium mariscus*) capable of surviving only with constantly submerged root systems. The fertile, flooded levee banks, like the winding streams and floodplain edges of the Panhandle to the north, support two types of plant life: grasses and reeds (*Phragmites australis, P. mauritianus, Miscanthus junceus*) rooted in the stronger currents on the outside of the bends, and softer sedges (*Cyperus papyrus, C. articulatus*) which predominate along the inner, shallower, slower flowing sides.

Islands, formed around termite mounds built on once dry plains or on channel sands, combined with the relatively stable water level, provide solid support for abundant tree life, especially along the island perimeters. Wild date palms characteristically ring the edges. The tall slender plants have crowns of almost luminous green fronds on stems ribbed with two rows of rapier-

Poling looks easy, but like any art takes practice. And a compass doesn't help either.

Late home run.

like thorns. Extremely hydrophilic, they have fully submerged root systems, but need to be anchored firmly in solid ground. The water sometimes wears away the soil along the outside bends of strong-flowing channels until these picturesque palms topple.

Garcinia, Diospyros and *Ficus* (especially *F. burkei,* the contorted strangler fig parasite that eventually kills its host) are also found near these palms. The thickly wooded zone supports arboreal squirrels, chacma baboons, vervet monkeys and what has been referred to as the bird with the 'screeching howl of a lost soul falling into a bottomless pit', Pel's fishing owl. The presence of the owl (*Scotopelia peli*) is otherwise revealed by small white fish scales in its droppings on the dead leaf cover below the African mangosteen (*Garcinia livingstonei*), one of its favourite perches.

Yellowbilled kite (Milvus aegypticus), a scavenger and predator.

Death is as bleak on the sands of the Makgadikgadi Pans as on a river bed near the top of the seasonal swamp.

Wild date palms cover an entrance to an island in the permanent swamp.

Typical perch for a crocodile in the main channel.

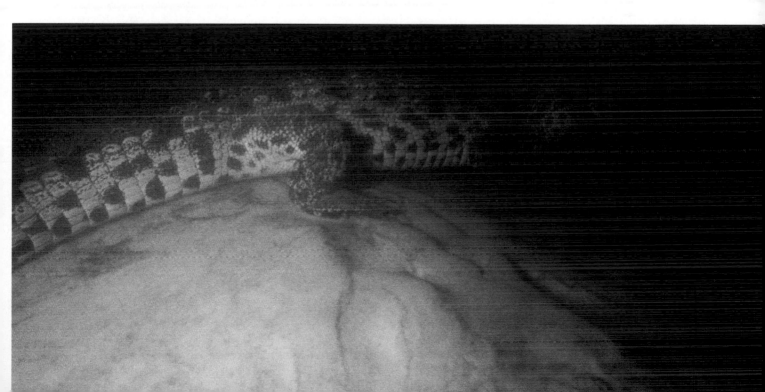

The fast-growing strangler fig (Ficus burkei) is common throughout the Delta and soon kills its host.

Growing up to 60 centimetres tall, this baby Pel's fishing owl (Scotopelia peli) ruffs its feathers in a mukotshomo tree (Diospyros mespiliformis) in an attempt to look larger and more forboding. Razor sharp sight and hearing makes it a deadly nocturnal hunter.

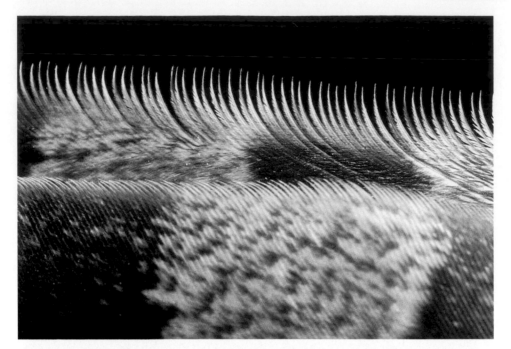

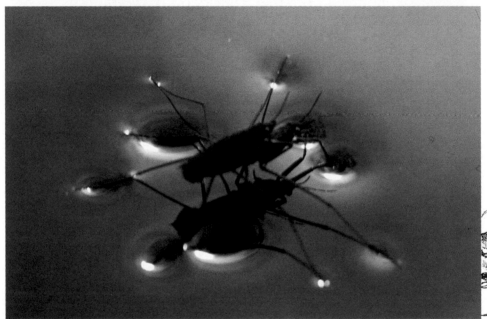

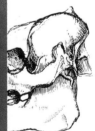

In the dry areas starting some 10 to 15 metres from the waterline, umbrella and camelthorn trees (*Acacia tortilis, A. erioloba*) and fan palms (*Hyphaenae ventricosa*) grow up to the edge of the grassy interior or floodplain sides of the islands.

Slow evaporation over thousands of years and constantly fluctuating water levels, combined with a rising and falling saline groundwater table, have left porous sand with a crust of white salts (mainly calcium, magnesium and sodium) on the island interiors. Despite bearing very low concentrations of dissolved material, the huge volume of flood water each year sweeps along some of the Delta's groundwater. The weight of the rising flood waters also slightly compresses the sedimentation. To maintain hydrostatic equilibrium, the groundwater is squeezed up towards the surface, where the salts remain after evaporation has occurred. Only the hardiest of plants will tolerate the resultant soil, generally the tough rhizome-stemmed grass *Sporobolus*

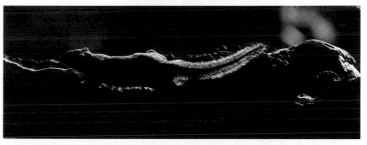

spicatus, though sometimes in association with leadwood trees (*Combretum imberbe*) and fan palms. Locally known as ntsongo, the grass has needle-sharp leaves, reflecting its hardy character. The white salts are often drawn onto the plant by capillary action, resulting in a white, spiky, crystalline appearance. The salts will burn the bare flesh, especially when wet with early morning dew. It is from these salts that termites obtain the small calcite crystals used in the construction of their mounds on the islands.

The channels and lagoons are rimmed with papyrus, and as the Delta is primarily explored by boat, it is often mistakenly thought to be the dominant plant in this section of the swamp. Papyrus distribution is governed by water fluctuations and dissolved salt levels. Their roots and rhizomes must be in perennial contact with fresh water, either floating or permanently submerged. These conditions only exist along the margins of open, stable water — the channels and lagoons of the permanent swamp. While the floodplains are mostly grassed, some of the lower lying sections may support a mixed community of grasses (*Phragmites australis*), other sedges, papyrus, the bullrush (*Typha latifolia*) and smaller ferns (*Thelypterus* sp), though never patches of pure papyrus.

The leading edge of a giant eagle owl's (Bubo lacteus) wing stops the air whistling at it swoops.

The weight of this water strider (Amphibicorisae mesoveliidae) is not enough to break the surface tension and it can walk quite dryly over water.

Ntsongo (Sporobolus spicatus) outcompetes most other species on the salt-flushed island sections.

Getting started.

A tree squirrel (Paraxerus cepapi) bolsters its image. Size can mean the difference between being hunted and left alone.

Crocodiles use the sun, water and their mouths to regulate their body temperature.

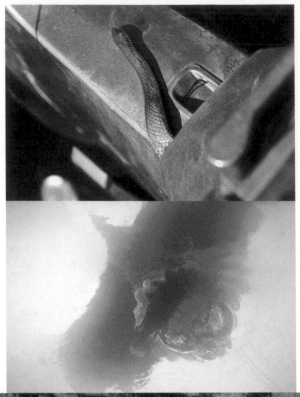

An olive marsh snake (Natriciteres olivaceo) *seeking warm shelter for the night received a rude shock the following morning. So did the driver!*

One of the hundreds of remote underwater pictures that did not work.

Water mirrors images both above and below its surface.

Perspective of the swamp's first public bar.

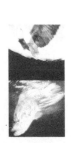

A simple juxtaposition portrays two kinds of adrenalin.

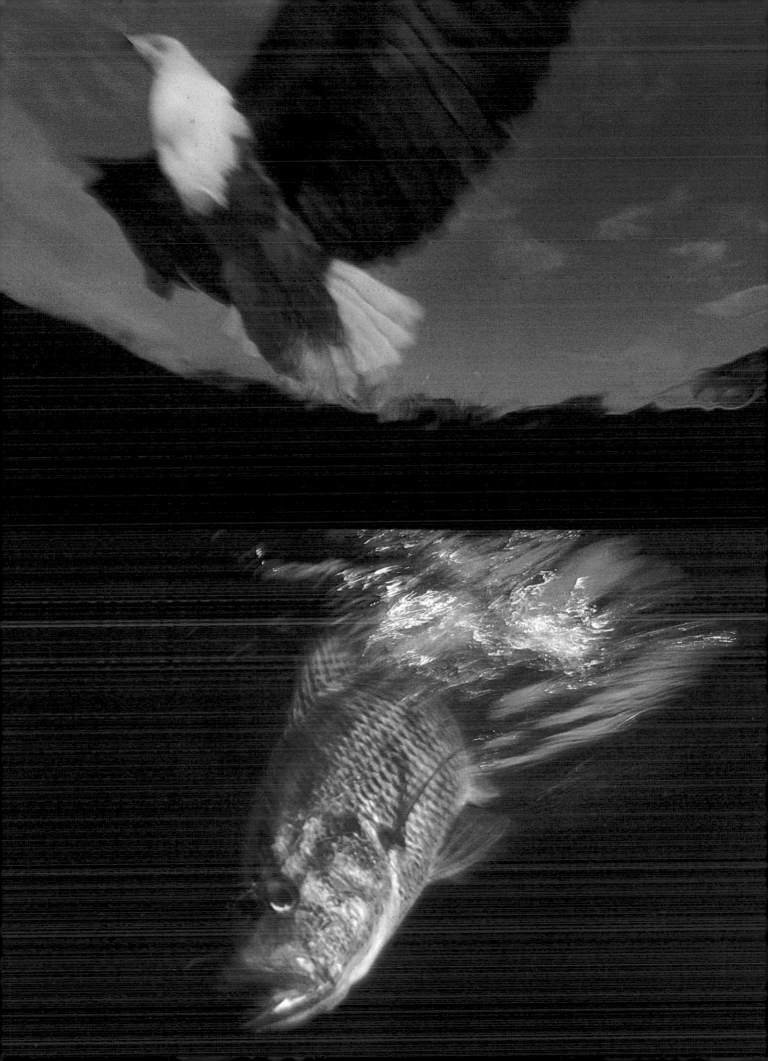

Despite the notoriously poor nutrient conditions of the Okavango waters, papyrus uses rapid C4 photosynthetic pathways and recycles nutrients from old growth within the plant itself so efficiently that its rate of propagation compares favourably with that found in intensive agriculture where all conditions are artificially optimised. ('C4' plants produce more glucose for a given leaf area than 'C3' plants and consequently grow faster. They also do not exhibit photorespiration, a form of daylight respiration that can reduce energy conversion levels by up to 50 per cent.)

The rate of growth of papyrus is roughly balanced with breakage and attrition by fire and grazing, though excessive growth as well as attrition have been noted in local communities.

Papyrus stalks torn from community perimeters combined with floating debris and rhizomes growing across slow-flowing streams often form dense blockages in the permanent swamp. These blockages are 'self-propagating': as the decaying mat of trapped vegetation grows thicker, sedimentation increases as the water velocity decreases, and more of the current-borne nutrients are able to reach roots anchored high on the levee banks, thus encouraging the growth of even more potentially blocking vegetation.

While the banks are often too well protected by tightly woven papyrus to suffer erosion and subsequent changes in channel direction, the plant, in conjunction with a greater cycle of tectonic activity, plays a major part in modifying the distribution of the water.

The Thaoge River, once the Delta's main western distributary, and described by David Livingstone late last century as 'gushing' into Lake Ngami, has become a completely constricted papyrus bog. Flow registers taken before and after a local earthquake in 1952 reveal a major change in water volume and

Only the ripples reveal the presence of crystal-clear water flowing over sedges in a shallow plain.

Channels must frequently be cleared of drifting, matted vegetation, particularly broken papyrus.

Storing a full petrol drum for a return journey from the Panhandle.

Eighty-four species of fish are known to exist in the Delta, and more are being discovered each year.

There is more to death than birds of prey and aquatic predators. Greenhead tilapia (Oreochromus macrochir).

AFRIQUE

velocity. The river now disappears half way down its course beneath a thick, spongy papyrus mat, mostly solid enough to walk on, but with parts soft enough for one to sink into forever.

Confined to the waters of the permanent swamp and Panhandle by shallow, grassy 'flats' over which the water must pass to the seasonal swamp, are the predatory tiger fish. Outnumbering the largemouthed bream (*Serranochromis* spp), and other fish like the African pike (*Hepsetus odoe*) more numerous in the lower Delta, the tiger fish thrives in the clear, fast-flowing and deeper channels.

The more notorious predators of the area, crocodiles, are often found on papyrus and island banks or lurking on channel floors, and seem larger than in the lower Delta. It is possible that commercial hunting (more than 10 000 were killed between 1957 and 1969) was less extensive in the permanent swamp, where crocodiles are not restricted to the navigable channels when the annual flood is at its lowest ebb.

Also found here is the extremely shy and relatively scarce sitatunga antelope. Its elongated, semi-flexible hooves are specially adapted to a swamp environment and enable it to walk through and over papyrus beds, particularly those floating on channel and lagoon margins, giving it access to resources inaccessible to other grazers. Grazing in the early morning and evening on papyrus umbels, grasses, sedges and the foliage of trees, sitatunga live solitary lives, though sometimes females can be found in groups. They have been seen grazing with red lechwe (*Kobus leche*) as well. Because of their habits they need fear no land-based predators, though there have been rare instances of lion kills. Okavango lore tells of the monotonous regularity of this animal's life, to the point that 'you can set your watch by sitatunga supper time'!

Nile crocodile
(Crocodilus niloticus)

'Drifting along underwater strapped to an aqualung tank and taking photographs, I floated to my horror over a crocodile much larger than myself. My head was already above its back legs and my feet over its head before I realised that the odd pattern on the river bed was the scales on the reptile's back! One is told to freeze. You don't even have to remember. You do it automatically. The current carried me over the rest of the body while I tried desperately to resist the temptation to kick with my flippers and speed away. The crocodile remained motionless — apparently trying to remain unseen. It was our first chance at an underwater picture. From what I thought was a safe distance, I turned and clicked the shutter button, and flash! The crocodile fled. So did I. If it had been a hippo I think the outcome would have been very different.' *(BOB FORRESTER)*

Crocodiles, survivors of the Cretaceous period 64 million years ago, do not lie constantly in wait for any morsel to chance by and then attack impulsively. They have very specific hunting patterns and do not need large amounts of food. They are shy creatures, and normally choose to retreat from difficult situations. They are not cold-blooded, as is commonly thought. Being reptiles, they need to spend much time in the sun to absorb the warmth needed to raise their body temperatures. This lack of an internal heating system means they rarely hunt early in the morning, after the cool of the night. In energy-sapping cold water, crocodiles may even drown. The Yei, a tribe in the north-western part of the swamp, claim that a crocodile's teeth are 'blunt in winter'.

Interestingly, heat is also necessary to activate the enzymes in the crocodile's digestive tract. Lack of sunshine hinders digestion, which may result in the animal being poisoned by food decaying in its stomach. Like man, the crocodile has pressure sensors in its jaws, and can determine the degree of force needed to close its mouth. These sense organs are so finely tuned that it is believed they even have the ability to sense atmospheric pressure, and when the pressure drops before a rainstorm, a crocodile will generally not eat, thereby avoiding poisoning.

Making maximum use of natural warming elements, crocodiles spend their nights in the water, which loses heat more slowly than land does.

As they are often seen lying with their mouths wide open, displaying their fearsome-looking teeth, it is thought that the blood circulating in the tongue may help to regulate heat, much as an elephant's ears do.

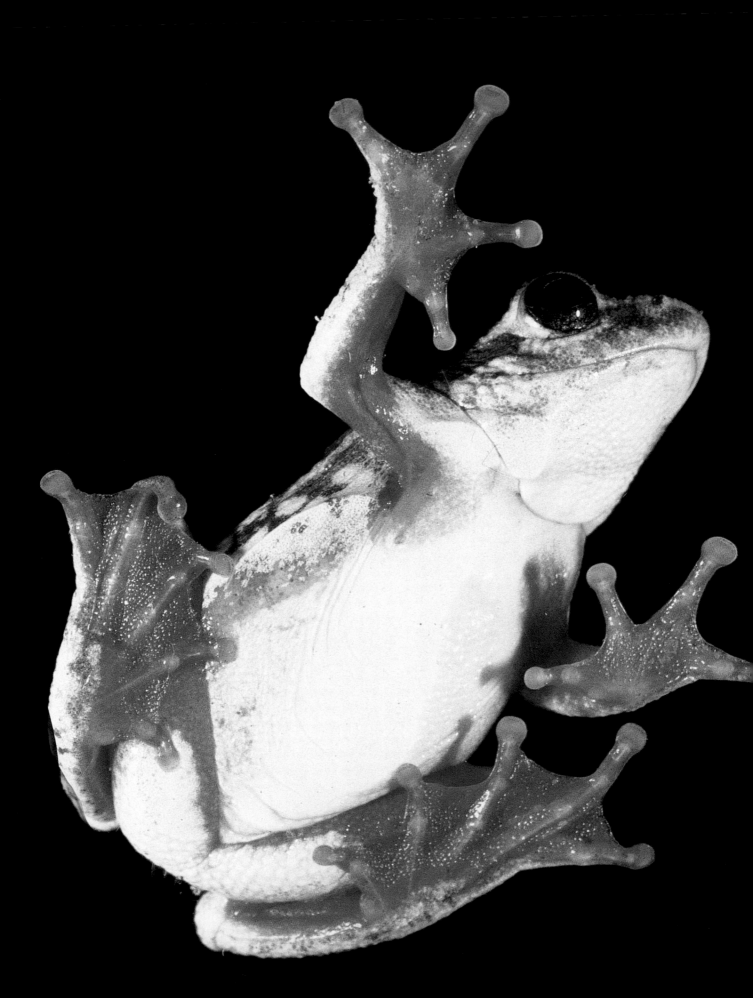

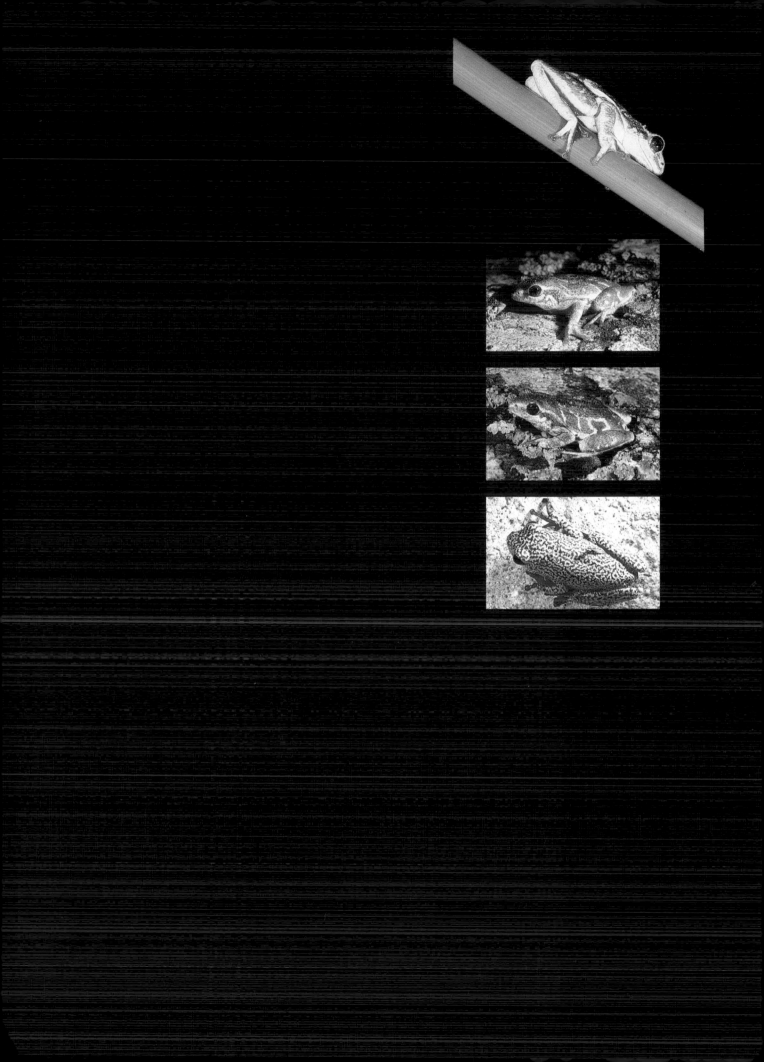

Botswana's flat horizons force one's eyes skyward. A typical cloud build-up in the early rainy season.

Painted reed frog (Hyperolius marmoratus) splayed, and on sedge stem, changes colour for camouflage protection.

Life on the heels of the high tide

The seasonal swamp

'There were once many animals, many, many. And we hunted freely. Now hunting is strictly controlled, and many animals have gone. I'm not sure why.'

BATSELELWENG SENKAPAU. SWAMPER, b. 1929

'Even as I write now my mind is pleasantly excited at the marvellous sight of game that bursts on my view. As far as I could see up the open laagte the ground was teeming with heavy game. Close in front of me stood three giraffes; a little further on a troop of seven more; between these a group of buffalo; a little beyond, troops of giraffe, eland, buffalo, hartebeest, quagga, letswee, reed buck, blue wildebeest, ostriches, rooi buck, and more, and more . . . Unable to control myself from excitement . . . I guiltily clinked the nearest giraffe sixty yards off under the ear with a Martini-Henry bullet.'

AUREL SCHULZ, EXPLORER, 1897

The annual flood waters from Angola surge into the Panhandle and permanent swamp in a sustained rush. Progressively the funnel of the Delta opens wider, gradients lessen and vegetation becomes more dense as the wave reaches the seasonal swamp. Here the water seeps across sun-dried floodplains, soaking into sandy soils, down smaller and slower tributaries, trickling through stream beds that arc otherwise parched for most of the year.

The initial thrust of the flood, surging ahead of the main volume close behind, may raise channel water levels by nearly one metre overnight.

The water is turbulent and dark with organic matter flushed from summer-stagnant floodplains. The rise continues for one to two months, depending on the length and extent of the Angolan rainfall season six months previously. This massive influx of water, in conjunction with the low relief, increases the area of submerged land enormously.

The channels fill until levee banks disappear, with gentle ripples on the surface of the water the only clue to the aggrading banks' existence. The neighbouring floodplains are gradually replenished, and a slight rise is visible each day. As these seasonal swamp plains become inundated, so the water level in the upper Panhandle drops in response to the trough left by the southward-flowing crest, cutting neighbouring floodplains off from the main channel.

The life-giving flood crest rippling across the Delta triggers a period of frenetic growth in aquatic plants like the broad-leafed water lily (*Nymphaea capensis*), the bulbs of which have waited out the dry summer months beneath the silt. Reproductive cycles must be completed before the peak of the flood passes and the water recedes. Phytoplankton (microscopic plants) and algae take immediate advantage of the incoming water, soaking up dissolved nutrients not yet absorbed by rooted vegetation. Stems of emergent aquatic vegetation soon serve as anchors for the gelatinous green fronds of spyrogyra and other simple plants.

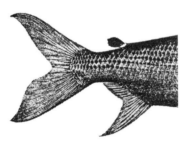 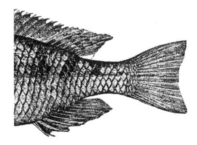

As the floodplains grow shallow toward the trees that mark the edge of the high-water level, aquatic plants give way to sedges (*Cyperus articulatus, C. denudata*), until grasses (*Panicum repens, Imperata cylindrica*) eventually dominate, revealing a distinct zoning pattern determined by each species' water requirements.

This sprouting vegetation — coveted grazing — as well as dry summer grasses and established growth, now become accessible to a variety of aquatic animals, many of which have spent months confined to relatively barren, sandy channels.

Zooplankton and filter-feeding insect larvae glean a living from the phytoplankton and suspended detritus, while larger scavengers roam the floodplain floors. Nocturnal bottle-nose mormyrids (*Mormyrops* sp) closely related to the mormyrids that are savaged during the catfish

Forests of weed sway to and fro.

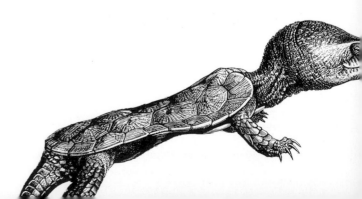

runs, navigate by means of electric fields in their search for insect larvae, molluscs and algae. The opportunistic, largely nocturnal catfish seeks frogs (*Rana* spp) and small fish (*Schilbe mystus, Barbus* sp) while numerous grazers like snails (*Biomphalaria* spp) and red-breasted bream (*Tilapia rendalli rendalli*) feed on the algae, grasses and sedges. Pygmy geese (*Nettapus auritus*) forage for seeds.

The carnivorous bladderwort plant, *Utricularia,* restricted to still and slow-flowing ponds of permanent water, traps minute aquatic animals in specially evolved feeding pods. Touch stimulated, the pods close around any prey that brushes against them. The snared food is subsequently broken down by acids and absorbed, yielding important nitrogen.

Insects and rodents ousted from the flooded plains are another major food source for the numerous predators — fish, frogs, snakes, birds and small reptiles.

Many fish make use of the freshly filled melapo (floodplains) as a refuge from predators, and as feeding grounds.

The nocturnal mormyrid (Mormyrus lacerda) *is almost blind and generates an electronic field to navigate, feed and to detect the presence of other fish.*

To construct a mokoro, a tree must be chosen, felled and the upper half cut into V segments, which are then chipped away. The exterior and interior are fashioned with axe and adze only. The mokoro is essential for travel and the setting of nets to feed families. They are generally hewn from sausage trees, jakkalsbessies, water figs, mukwa and marula trees (Kigelia africana, Diospyrus mespilliformis, Ficus sycamorus, Pterocarpus angolensis *and* Slerocarya birrea).

Angular hamerkop (Scopus umbretta).

A hungry crocodile uses the backs of adult hippos to make a dash for a calf. The adults quickly formed a tight laager around the juvenile and by snapping at the crocodile with their huge jaws, drove the reptile off.

There is often no clear distinction between wet and dry, where islands begin and end.

Melapo are also ideal for breeding — the water flow is sufficient to carry decomposed plant nutrients to the small fry, but not strong enough to wash the young away. Some of the bream (cichlid) species build nursery 'arenas' comprising a number of holes up to 60 centimetres deep, grouped in a circular arrangement, in which their eggs are laid, fertilised and guarded by the parents. After hatching, the fry are tended until they are ready to fend for themselves.

Crocodile eggs are laid 30 to 40 centimetres deep early in summer and hatch just prior to the flood. The youngsters call from within the eggs with a sound that can be heard up to 20 metres away. Should they be unable to dig themselves free, the mother excavates the clutch and carries the hatched crocodiles in her mouth to the water.

Male crocodiles have been noted to roll the eggs gently back and forth on their tongues to induce hatching when the young are unable to crack open the shells. The young reptiles enjoy a certain amount of parental care, and spend their first few months in the relative safety of shallow water, after which they are fair game for the appetites of their elders. A good supply of crabs, insects, plants and frogs keep the juveniles well fed.

Slowly the tide turns and the pulse of the flood grows weaker.

A brooding bream (Tilapia sparrmanii) guards her green eggs.

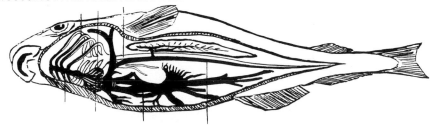

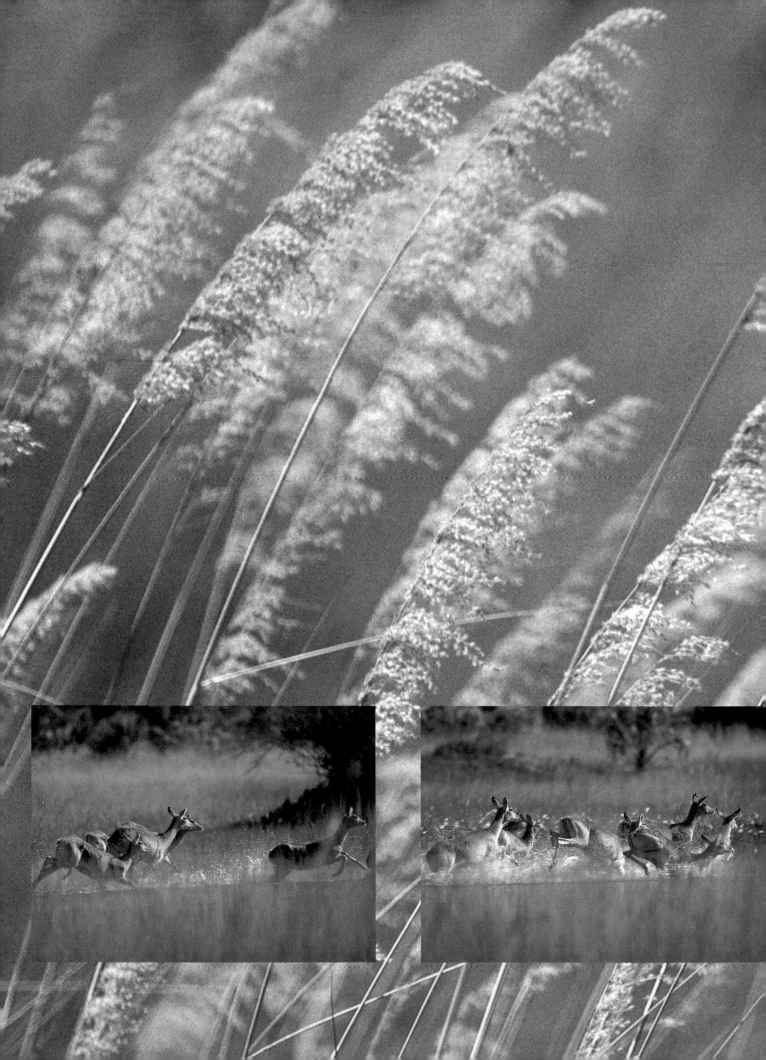

In early spring, as the water begins to recede from the seasonal swamp, the rain clouds build up again in Angola for the summer rainfall. The many aquatic animals of the flood period slowly emerge from the shelter and feeding grounds of the floodplains. Fish begin moving back into the channels and upstream in search of deeper water, as do reptiles and some amphibians. Some terrapins and toads, however, choose to wait for the next flood by burying themselves in the drying floodplain floor, aestivating through the dry months.

A large variety of birds patiently follows the receding edge of the flood water down the Delta throughout the year for this steadily growing concentration of food. Each species exploits a specific area of the floodplain as it becomes exposed. Flocks of openbilled storks (*Anastomus lamelligerus*) feed voraciously for a few weeks, followed by saddlebilled and woollynecked storks (*Ephippiorhynchus senegalensis, Ciconia episcopus*) and the rarer wattled crane (*Grus carunculata*).

Prior to the arrival of these waders, ducks (whitefaced and yellowbilled) and pygmy geese gorge themselves paddling and diving between the sedges and water grasses.

Then the massacre begins.

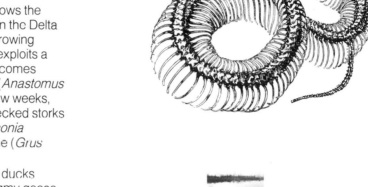

A rare misty dawn at peak flood half way up the seasonal swamp.

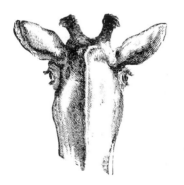 

The water level drops below the floodplain banks, leaving hundreds of fish trapped in evaporating pools. Large congregations of herons, egrets, stork and ibis line the edges of the pools and move steadily forward through the water, bills and beaks dipping frantically to withdraw silvery flashes. There is a flurry of movement and dozens of flapping fish are left stranded and exhausted on the banks.

Generally a carrion feeder, the marabou stork (*Leptoptilos crumeniferus*) is an inelegant and rather unattractive attendant at the feast. This bald-headed, smelly bird, which pokes its head into rotting carcasses, is often found at the edge of almost dry melapo where catfish have been left stranded and thrashing about in the mud.

This saddlebilled stork (Ephippiorhynchus senegalensis) caught the terrapin in a receding summer floodplain pan and then carried it out of sight.

Water lily leaves need no support structure from their stems to float on the water and catch the sun's rays.

While fairly plentiful, terrapins are difficult to detect.

Like cats, this squeaker (Synodontis sp) has whiskers (barbels) to guide itself around on nocturnal forages.

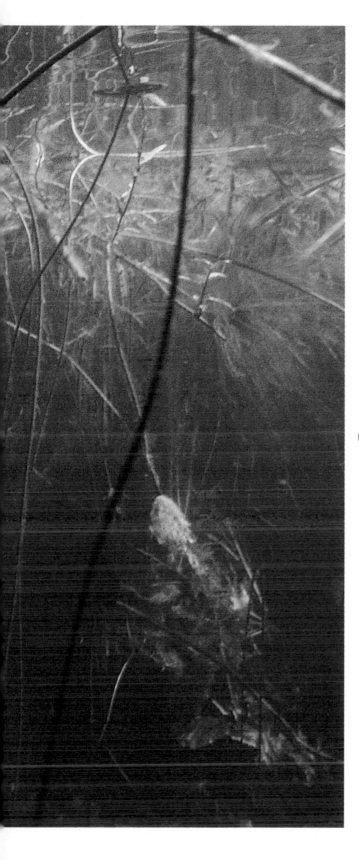

Crabs are the largest crustaceans in the Delta.

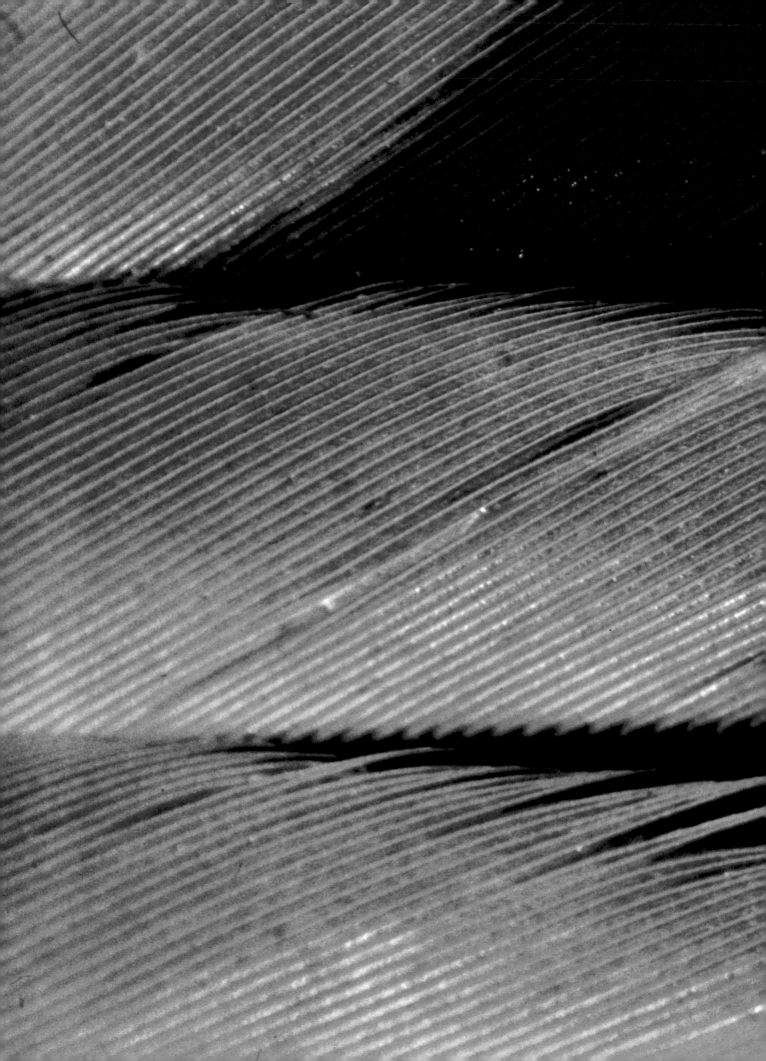

A double frame camera is used vertically.

Feather of lilacbreasted roller (Coralias caudata).

Reflections of the Delta from a high circling aircraft.

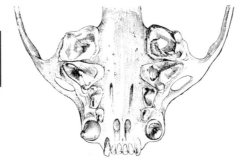

Pied kingfisher (Ceryle rudis), the hovering bird of the Okavango.

Pied and golden-blue malachite kingfishers (*Ceryle rudis, Alcedo cristata*) flutter from overhanging branches, and plunge into the water for a meal of cyprinid and characid fish; this small species also feeds on large spiders and catfish. The pied kingfisher is an incomparable aviator, hovering some six metres above the water, neck stretched downwards, until it becomes a black and white speckled blur, dive-bombing its target. It has a rather low success ratio — approximately one catch out of ten attempts — so it is often seen on the wing, energetically awaiting another insect or fish.

The gilled and reptilian predators are not left out of the feast. Slow-moving vegetarian and detritivorous fish that escaped the now isolated floodplains are forced to congregate in fast-flowing water offering little food or cover against nocturnal attacks by catfish and crocodile — the latter activated by warm spring temperatures. By day, razor-toothed pike and predatory bream hungrily cruise the channels, though ever watchful for the swooping shadows of cormorants, herons and fish eagles. By night, the large, secretive fishing owl perches patiently in the trees after its dusk hunting activities.

Clawed and Cape clawless otters (*Lutra maculicollis, Aonyx capensis*) bob and arch gracefully with deceptive speed through the streams in search of fish, frogs and insects. Their strong jaws and dexterous front limbs also enable them to eat mussels and crabs, whose hard shells make them inaccessible to most other aquatic carnivores. The decreasing force of the flood allows the remaining silt to settle, which in time forms mud strata of fine sediment mainly derived from termite mounds, through which the water eventually cuts and where vegetation may take root. Mussels, confined to channels with year-round flow, can be found in sandbanks in this spongy clay, filtering debris from the passing water. While few plants are equipped to deal with the midstream current — the mobile sand bedload makes anchorage difficult — some grow in the thicker sand, and others in the protected lees of sandy bays.

Red lechwe in the northern sector of the seasonal swamp.

Buffalo (Syncerus caffer) disturbed while grazing.

Red lechwe make their way across the floodplain.

Animals, like mechanical vehicles, leave a distinct, long-lasting trail.

Frequent Okavango visitors provide their own form of capped merriment.

Author and Lesajwa, the guide, at home around the kitchen stove.

Milk plays a prominent role in the diets of young warthogs (Phacochoerus aethiopicus).

Tall grasses like the dense *Miscanthus junceus* line the channel banks, which are often completely exposed at ebb times. Water lilies, prolific in the floodplains, are confined to the quieter waters inside the river bends of the swirling streams.

The recession of the flood in the lower section of the Delta is greatly accelerated during the last dry months prior to the start of the rainy season. The lush vegetation and diminishing surface area of the still moist, though abandoned floodplains are dehydrated increasingly by the dry, scorching winds and sun of September and October, known to Ngamilanders as the 'suicide months' — with

stifling temperatures of up to 44 °C. Water lilies and other aquatics die back to give way to new grasses and sedges, mostly good grazing plants adapted to their environment, able to convert sunshine into enough energy to complete the reproductive cycle before the start of the rainy season. This rapidly growing vegetation synchronised with the final regression of the water down the floodplain slopes, is vital to the grazing communities.

During the high-water period resident grazers are forced inland to the sparsely grassed, though essentially arid, islands and to the greener, narrow zone between the treeline and the high-

White people say zebra (Equus burchelli) are white with black stripes. Black people are adamant the animals are black with white stripes!

water line. Should the water remain high, constant pressure on the lush zone would result in overgrazing. The receding water, however, progressively exposes new patches of fast-growing C4 plants, thus eliminating the danger of any zone being overgrazed. This danger is further averted in the long term by the variation in the extent and distribution of flooding from year to year, ensuring that the peak flood grazing line changes annually.

Shallow reflection from mid-stream.

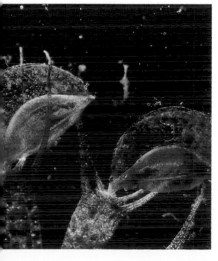

Butterfly's wing.

Insect covered insect.

Unidentified carapace.

Utricularia, a carnivorous aquatic plant, with its prey in a touch-sensitive feeding pod.

Reed cormorants line the waterways of the swamp.

Pygmy geese in their favourite slow-flowing, lily-covered habitat. And another in flight.

Wattled crane (Grus carunculata), wary and difficult to approach.

106

Grasses and sedges grow throughout the flooded melapo, from the centres right up to and into the treeline. Small aquatic herbivores forage here, as well as water-loving mammals; hippo, buffalo (*Syncerus caffer*) and lechwe are often found grazing hock deep, nipping off the tender shoots. When the water has receded enough, the plains animals like tsessebe (*Damaliscus lunatus*) and impala (*Aepyceros melampus*) take their turn. The young, green shoots receive little protection. *Panicum repens*, a hydrophilic grass, is valuable fodder for buffalo as the water recedes, and is also eaten extensively from below by red-breasted bream when the flood waters are high. On the dry floodplains, warthog (*Phacochoerus aethiopicus*) root out rhizomes and tubers, often in the company of baboons, who wisely leave most of the digging to the pigs.

The bill of the sacred ibis is perfect for probing the shallows and mud for food.

The saddlebilled stork deploys similar wader feeding strategies to the marabou and ibis.

The marabou stork plunders the receding floodplains for fleeing fish.

Wattled cranes (Grus carunculata) *patrol the water's edge.*

Warthogs, some of the largest mammals to dig for food, often clear large areas of earth with their upper tusks. Their lower tusks, constantly honed to near razor sharpness against their upper digging partners, are formidable weapons, and few carnivores, including lion (*Panthera leo*), will dare attack them.

A cormorantry is well-protected from land-based predators.

Adult reed cormorant slowly scans the horizon for danger.

An unidentified flock, probably openbilled stork (Anastomus lamelligerus), *wheels across the sky during a seasonal migration.*

Repairs at the base camp dock.

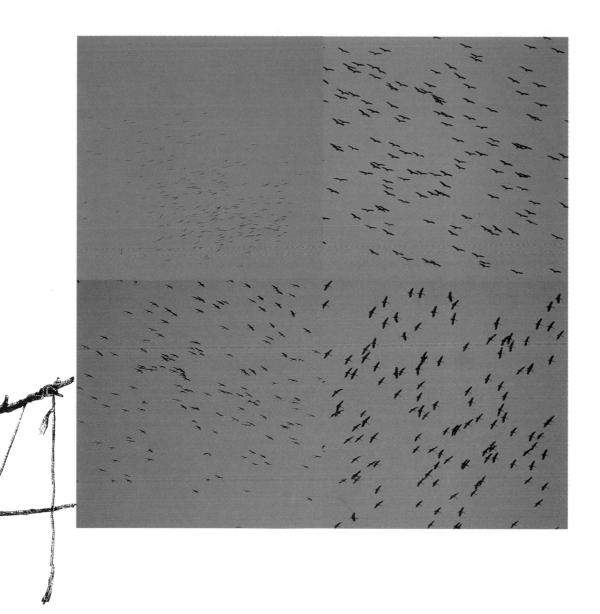

The summer rains help maintain the water volume while the drying, hot summer sun is at its keenest, and a number of shallow rain pools exist over a large area for a short time. As summer draws to an end, and the many pans in the arid, peripheral lands dry up, more grazers move in toward the receding swamp margins. Large herds of Burchell's zebra (*Equus burchelli*) and black wildebeest (*Connochaetes gnou*) move in search of water through the dry months that follow.

The grazers in their turn sustain the land-based predators. Spotted hyaena (*Crocuta crocuta*) and leopard (*Panthera pardus*) are often found within the boundaries of the swamp, while lion prefer to hunt on the marginal floodplains, between the swamp and the large, dry land masses — Chief's Island and the 'sandveld' tongues.

Zebra are regular targets for lion attacks.

Their black and white stripes, commonly accepted as camouflage markings, have also been considered an aid to escape. As the herd runs from a predator, the moving stripes are thought to make it difficult to distinguish between separate animals, forcing the hunter to pursue stragglers or strays instead of driving into the pack.

Spotted hyaena prefer to hunt not too far from the water, and enjoy the occasional swim. They have been seen killing lechwe by drowning the victim. Inside the Delta, they move around in small groups, or solitarily, as opposed to the clans of the savannah.

The flood is the life-line for the water-dependent animals. For the rest of the year they range far afield in search of temporary pans in the mopane forests and thornveld. Should the floods cease, they, along with much of the vegetation, would perish.

Chacma baboon
Papio ursinus chobiensis

Whatever anthropologists and zoologists may say, our fascination with baboons surely lies in their likeness to man. So different, yet so similar. Their lively social chatter, possessive maternal behaviour, and the swamp troops' languid eating habits, are all too familiar.

The Okavango swamp is perfectly suited to baboons. Abundant food and a relatively low predation rate have resulted in a large number of troops, each of which can consist of up to a hundred members. Leopards are their main enemies, and often take a heavy toll on their numbers, but seem to act more as a natural control against overpopulation than to pose any real threat to the baboons' existence. It is generally the older, slower or weaker baboons that are preyed upon, and their eradication gives the troop added mobility and strength.

Like humans, baboons are omnivorous and opportunistic feeders. While not active hunters, they do sometimes kill small buck and birds, but mostly eat fruit, roots, bulbs, seeds, leaves, grasses, berries and insects. Humans, too, have an enzyme in their stomachs to digest insects!

Historically, man's hierarchies have depended on the ability to outwit, outfight, outsmart or outface an opponent. So too with baboons, who are strictly governed by a certain pecking order. The leader, the dominant male, is the one who successfully wards off opposing troop members. His position is often retained through a number of mock attacks, but is won initially in physical combat, though baboons rarely fight to the death. When he eventually loses, other males often join in the challenge, and he may quickly fall to the fifth, sixth or seventh rung in the hierarchy. The dominant male is also the sole progenitor, thus ensuring that the strongest strains are passed on to the offspring.

Females, too, form a hierarchical structure, though theirs is based on inheritance: daughters of dominant mothers become dominant adults.

Baboons seem to have a vehement dislike of crossing water and will strip an area of food before deciding to move. The troop will take to trees overhanging the water to be crossed and agitatedly gaze at the next island, until one by one they attempt to jump across, no matter how far. They inevitably fall into the water and scurry across the shallows, attempting at all costs to keep even the tips of their tails dry, acting with great indignation should they get them wet.

113

Chacma baboons keep watch over feeding troops from termitaria and trees. While on the mounds, they often spend hours enticing termites out of their holes with a long blade of grass. The termites are rapidly devoured.

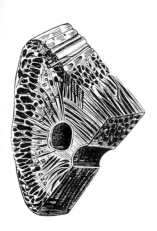

The ventilation shaft of a termite ant (Macrotermes michaelseni) *colony.*

We taught an orphan juvenile yellowbilled kite to fly, and it never returned.

Cape glossy starling (Lamprotornis nitens), sometimes blue, sometimes black.

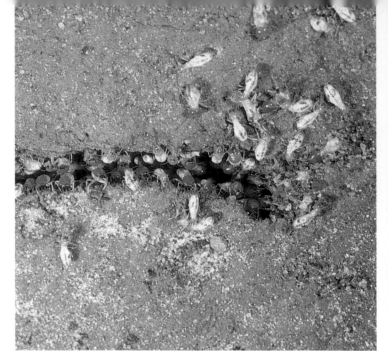

Irregular chains of islands form when termites build mounds near old colonies.

The termite is responsible for the construction of the mounds found on nearly every island, and around which many islands — other than those caused by change in channel direction — seem to grow. Each mound is, or was, the castle of a termite colony.

While each colony is functionally divided into four castes (reproductives, supplementary reproductives, soldiers and workers), some scientists consider the termite mound (or beehive) to be a single living entity, so specialised and interdependent are the parts. The queen is analogous to the sexual organs and the workers to the blood cells. If one termite is separated from the rest of the colony or body it dies. It needs only one successful pair of reproductive termites, purposefully released from their parent colony, to found a new colony and mound. Their release is closely synchronised with the first heavy rains following the dry season, when large areas of dry land in the Delta are available for colonisation. These reproductives or alates — commonly known as flying ants — have wings enabling them to fly far enough to avoid overcrowding and competition from other termites. They are even genetically prevented from breeding successfully until flying has occurred. Thousands upon thousands of alates are seasonally released to make up for a mortality rate that seems close to genocide.

A newly emerged alate ready for her virgin flight.

Soldier ants preparing an exit for alates, just prior to the first rains.

Heavy clay sediment builds up to eventually form flood strata.

African bees (Apis mellifera) *are important vectors of fertilisation for vegetation that does not fertilise itself or rely on wind. Insect-pollinated plants are often complex, with highly colourful and scented flowers to attract the insects, which in turn spread the pollen over a wide area.*

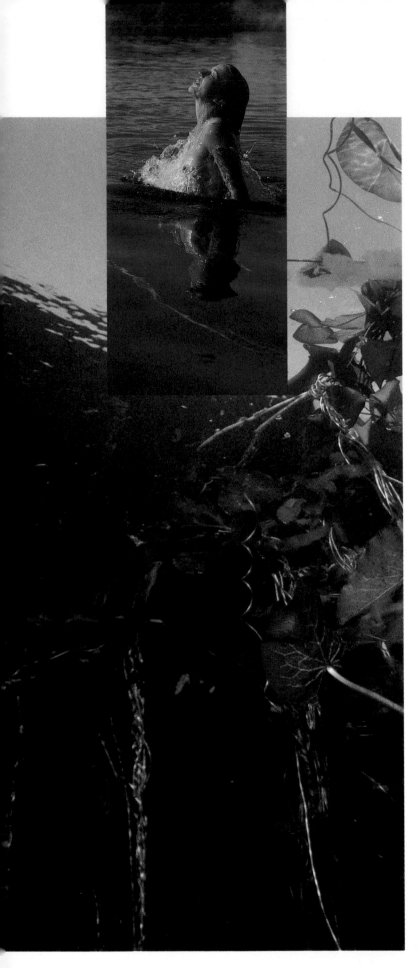

The instant they leave the mound they are gorged upon by frogs, toads, snakes, lizards, rats, cats and even jackals. In the air they fall prey to a host of insectivorous birds, from bee-eaters to kites, wheeling across the sky in a rampant feeding frenzy. The few survivors eventually land and shed their wings. Hopefully a few females will survive, who then emit a gaseous scent to attract a mate. Each pair searches for a suitable site to colonise, and if they survive the waiting ground predators again, which now include battalions of scurrying ants, they excavate a small hole and seal themselves in to breed.

From this pair will grow a colony, containing hundreds of thousands of termites, that may survive for up to 80 years. An extensive system of subterranean tunnels is excavated by a burgeoning worker force, and includes a well for water, tunnels for food collection, and chambers for fungus collection (the ant is the only animal other than man to harbour agricultural instincts, cultivating fungus for feeding its larvae). An extremely sophisticated ventilation system keeps temperatures and humidity at an optimum in and below the mound. The conspicuous spire plays a part in the ventilation of the nest, and is specifically designed to lean at the correct angle to ensure the right amount of exposure to the heat of the sun and to the cooling winds.

Spyrogyra clings and grows on stems and shoots.

In the dry months between the rainy summer and winter flood, the termite mounds appear in the middle of the dry floodplains, initially protruding perhaps half a metre above the peak water level. To regard them merely as blobs on the landscape is to belie their role in the dynamics of the swamp. They both contain life and generate it. Constructed from swamp sand, salts found on the islands, and clays from the floodplain sediments, the structures are 'cemented' together with termite saliva secreted from glands near the mandibles of the worker ants. Each grain of sand is rolled between the articulated mandibles, coated in saliva and set in precise place according to a plan engraved in the termites' genetic make-up.

The importance of the mound is that the concrete-like clay is harder and more persistent than any other substrata occurring in the Delta.

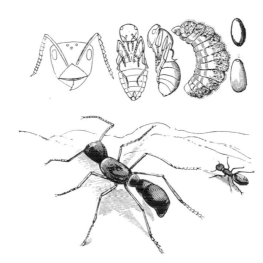

Acting as a barrier to the gently flowing floodplain water, sediment slowly forms a sloping base to the spire. Birds use the protrusion as a convenient perch and may deposit seeds from trees with fruit like *Garcinia* and *Diospyros* that may germinate and grow in the mound. The roots in turn strengthen the mound to withstand erosion, and the fallen leaves improve the nutritional content of the soil, making it even more hospitable for additional plant life. An embryonic island is formed, which will eventually support a greater variety of plants and animals — providing shelter and food where once only grasses and sedges grew. This colony in turn sends out its own alates, ultimately forming a chain of islands which may change the flow pattern of the floodplain. Small beginnings . . .

Checklists of common species

The Western European scientific tradition classifies fauna and flora under the Linnaean system, a formal framework which shows the similarities and differences between species and their evolutionary origins. The African seTswana system of classification is based upon functional use. Plants and animals which are important to traditional life are specifically named and identified.

Mammals

ENGLISH	SETSWANA	GENERIC
Antbear	Thakadu	*Orycteropus afer*
Baboon	Tswene	*Papio ursinus*
Bat-eared fox	Mothose	*Otocyon megalotis*
Buffalo	Nare	*Syncerus caffer*
Bushbuck	Ngurungu	*Tragelaphus scriptus*
Bush pig	Kolobe ea naga	*Potamochoerus porcus*
Cat (African wild)	Tibe	*Felis lybica*
Cat (Small spotted)	Sebalabolokwane	*Felis nigripes*
Cheetah	Letotse	*Acinonyx jubatus*
Civet (African)	Tshipalore	*Civettictis civetta*
Duiker (Common)	Phuti	*Sylvicapra grimmia*
Eland	Phofhu	*Taurotragus oryx*
Elephant	Tlou	*Loxodonta africana*
Galago (Bush baby)	Mogwele	*Galago senegalensis*
Genet (Small-spotted)	Tshipa	*Genetta genetta*
Genet (Large-spotted)	Tshipa	*Genetta tigrina*
Giraffe	Thutlwa	*Giraffa camelopardalis*

ENGLISH	SETSWANA	GENERIC
Hare (Scrub)	Mmutla	*Lepus saxatilis*
Hare (Spring)	Ntole	*Pedetes capensis*
Hippopotamus	Kubu	*Hippopotamus amphibius*
Honey badger	Matshwane	*Mellivora capensis*
Hyaena (Spotted)	Phiri	*Crocuta crocuta*
Impala	Phala	*Aepyceros melampus*
Jackal (Black-backed)	Phokoje	*Canis mesomelas*
Jackal (Side-striped)	Rantalaje	*Canis adustus*
Kudu	Tholo	*Tragelaphus strepsiceros*
Lechwe (Red)	Letsui	*Kobus leche*
Leopard	Nkwe	*Panthera pardus*
Lion	Tau	*Panthera leo*
Mongoose (Banded)	Letototo	*Mungos mungo*
Mongoose (Selous)	—	*Paracynictus selousi*
Mongoose (Yellow)	Moswe	*Cynictis penicillata*
Mongoose (Large grey)	—	*Herpestes ichneumon*
Mongoose (Slender)	Ngano	*Galerella sanguinea*
Mongoose (White-tailed)	—	*Ichneumia albicauda*
Mongoose (Water)	Tshagane	*Atilax paludinosus*
Mongoose (Dwarf)	Leswekete	*Helogale parvula*
Monkey (Vervet)	Kgabo	*Cercopithecus aethiops*
Otter (Cape clawless)	Kunyananoka	*Aonyx capensis*
Otter (Spotted-necked)	Kunyananoka	*Lutra maculicollis*
Pangolin	Kgaga	*Manis temminckii*
Porcupine	Noko	*Hystrix africaeaustralis*
Roan antelope	Kwalata etseta	*Hippotragus equinus*
Reedbuck	Sebogata	*Redunca arundinum*
Sable antelope	Kwalata entsho	*Hippotragus niger*
Serval	Thadi	*Felis serval*
Sitatunga	Naakong	*Tragelaphus spekei*
Squirrel	Sethora	*Paraxerus cepapi*
Steenbok	Phuduhudu	*Raphicerus campestris*
Tsessebe	Kabole	*Damaliscus lunatus*
Warthog	Kolobe	*Phacochoerus aethiopicus*
Waterbuck	Letemoga	*Kobus ellipsiprymnus*
Wild dog	Letharelwa	*Lycaon pictus*
Wildebeest (Blue)	Kgokong	*Connochaetes taurinus*
Zebra (Burchell's)	Pitse ea naga	*Equus burchelli*

Trees

ENGLISH	SETSWANA	GENERIC
Jackal-berry (606)*	Mokutshumo	*Diospyros mespiliformis*
Lowveld mangosteen (486)	Motsaudi	*Garcinia livingstonei*
Apple-leaf (238)	Mopororo	*Lonchocarpus capassa*
Baobab (467)	Moana	*Adansonia digitata*
Black thorn (176)	Mongana	*Acacia mellifera*
Brown ivory (449)	Mosintsela	*Berchemia discolor*
Plate thorn (165)	Mohahu	*Acacia fleckii*
Buffalo-thorn (447)	Mokgalo	*Ziziphus mucronata*
Rhodesian bushwillow (541)	Modubana	*Combretum collinum*
Candle thorn (170)	Setshi	*Acacia hebeclada*
Cape ash (298)	Motshai	*Ekebergia capensis*
Camel thorn (168)	Mogothlo	*Acacia erioloba*
Red spike-thorn (402)	Mothone	*Maytenus senegalensis*
Real fan palm (24)	Mokola	*Hyphaene petersiana*
Large fever-berry (329)	Motsebi	*Croton megalobotrys*
Flame thorn (160)	Mohukatau	*Acacia ataxacantha*
Transvaal gardenia (691)	Morala	*Gardenia folkensii*
Kalahari apple-leaf (239)	Mohadha	*Lonchocarpus nelsii*
Kalahari currant (393.2)	Morupaphiri	*Rhus tenuinervis*
Knobthorn (178)	Mokoba	*Acacia nigrescens*
Knobbly creeper (540.3)	Motswigitsane	*Combretum mossambicense*
Leadwood (539)	Motswiri	*Combretum imberbe*
Live-long (362)	Molebatsi	*Lannea discolor*
Magic guarri (595)	Mothlakola	*Euclea divinorum*
Marula (360)	Morula	*Sclerocarya birrea*
Manketti tree (337)	Mongongo	*Ricinodendron rautanenii*
Monkey thorn (166)	Mokala	*Acacia galpinii*
Mopane (198)	Mopane	*Colophospermum mopane*
Transvaal teak (236)	Mukwa	*Pterocarpus angolensis*
Common corkwood (285)	Siruka	*Commiphora pyracanthoides*
Paperbark thorn (187)	Morumusethla	*Acacia sieberiana*
Large-leaved falsethorn (158)	Mozindangoma	*Albizia versicolor*

ENGLISH	SETSWANA	GENERIC
Lowveld cluster-leaf (550)	Motshiara	*Terminalia prunioides*
Wild seringa (197)	Mosheshe	*Burkea africana*
Russet bushwillow (538)	Mokabi	*Combretum hereroense*
Sausage tree (678)	Moporota	*Kigelia africana*
Scented thorn (179)	Mothlabakgosi	*Acacia nilotica*
Shepherd's tree (122)	Motopi	*Boscia albitrunca*
Sickle bush (190)	Moselesele	*Dichrostachys cincrea*
Common false-thorn (155)	Molalakgaka	*Albizia harveyi*
Silver cluster-leat (551)	Mogonono	*Terminalia sericea*
Small sourplum (102)	Morutologa	*Ximenia americana*
Common wild fig (48)	Moumo	*Ficus burkei*
Sycamore fig (66)	Motshaba	*Ficus sycomorus*
Umbrella thorn (188)	Mushu	*Acacia tortilis*
River bitter tea (723.3)	Moqo	*Vernonia amygdalina*
Water fig (67.1)	Gomoti	*Ficus verruculosa*
Coffee neat's foot (208.3)	Mogutswe	*Bauhinia petersiana*
Wild date palm (22)	Tsaro	*Phoenix reclinata*
Rough-leaved raisin (459.2)	Mokgumphata	*Grewia flavescens*
Bastard raisin (458)	Moretlwa	*Grewia bicolor*
Water pear (557)	Qowa	*Syzygium guineense*
Woolly caper-bush (130.1)	Motawana	*Capparis tomentosa*

*Numbers from the SA *National List of Trees*. Also see Palgrave, KC, *Trees of Southern Africa*.

Sector of an inner swamp village, and an overgrazed homestead near Maun, the capital village of the region.

The malachite kingfisher, like the Okavango Delta, fragile and beautiful.

129

Amphibians and reptiles

ENGLISH	GENERIC
Frogs and toads	
Northern common platanna	*Xenopus laevis petersii*
Tropical platanna	*Xenopus muelleri*
Common toad	*Bufo gutturalis*
Northern mottled toad	*Bufo garmani*
Yellow swamp toad	*Bufo lemairi*
Red-banded frog	*Phrynomerus bifasciatus bifasciatus*
Common rain frog	*Breviceps adspersus*
Bullfrog	*Pyxicephalus adspersus adspersus*
Northern bullfrog	*Pyxicephalus a. edulis*
Cape sand frog	*Tomopterna cryptotis*
Knocking sand frog	*Tomopterna krugerensis*
Tropical grass frog	*Ptychadena subpunctata*
Sharp-nosed grass frog	*Ptychadena oxyrhynchus*
Mascarene grass frog	*Ptychadena m. mascareniensis*
Spotted-throated ridge frog	*Ptychadena taenioscelis*
Common puddle frog	*Phrynobatrachus natalensis*
Dwarf puddle frog	*Phrynobatrachus mababiensis*
Mottled shovel-nosed frog	*Hemisus marmoratum marmoratum*
Short-toed burrowing frog	*Hemisus guineensis microps*
Bubbling kassina	*Kassina senegalensis*
Sharp-nosed reed frog	*Hyperolius nasutus*
Painted reed frog	*Hyperolius marmoratus angolensis*

ENGLISH	GENERIC
Tortoises	
Leopard tortoise	*Geochelone pardalis babcocki*
Serrated tortoise	*Psammobates oculifer*

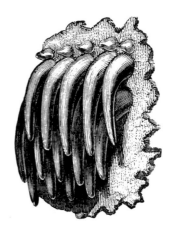

ENGLISH	GENERIC
Terrapins	
Marsh terrapin	*Pelomedusa subrufa*
Okavango hinged terrapin	*Pelusios bechuanicus bechuanicus*
Zimbabwe hinged terrapin	*Pelusios rhodesianus*
Crocodile	
Nile crocodile	*Crocodilus niloticus*
Gekkos	
Tropical house gekko	*Hemidactylus mabouia mabouia*
Bibron's gekko	*Pachydactylus bibronii*
Chobe dwarf gekko	*Lygodactylus chobiensis*
Agamas	
Tree agama	*Agama atricollis*
Kalahari agama	*Agama aculeata aculeata*
Peter's spiny agama	*Agama aculeata armata*
Chameleon	
Southern African chameleon	*Chamaeleo dilepis dilepis*

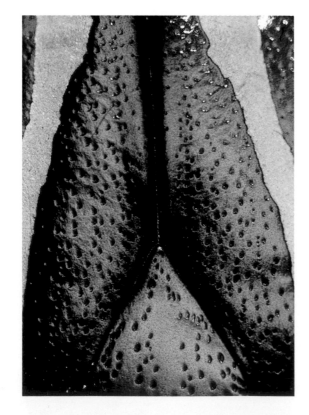

ENGLISH	GENERIC

Skinks

Ngami legless skink	*Typhlacontias gracilis rohani*
Sundeval's skink	*Lygosomas sundevalli sundevalli*
Mopani skink	*Mabuya striata wahlbergii*
Common variegated skink	*Mabuya varia*
Wahlberg's dwarf skink	*Afroablepharus wahlbergii*

Scincomorph lizards

Golden-plated lizard	*Gerrhosaurus multilineatus auritus*
Black-lined plated lizard	*Gerrhosaurus nigrolineatus nigrolineatus*

Lacertid lizards

Black-and-yellow sand lizard	*Heliobolus lugubris*
Rough-scaled sand lizard	*Ichnotropis squamulosa*
White-throated monitor	*Varanus exanthematicus albigularis*
Water monitor	*Varanus niloticus*

Snakes

Rock python	*Python sebae*
Brown house snake	*Lamprophis fuliginosus*
Mole snake	*Pseudaspis cana*
Olive marsh snake	*Natriciteres olivacea*
Eastern striped swamp snake	*Limnophis bicolor bangweolicus*
Striped skaapsteker	*Psammophylax tritaeniatus*
Eastern brown beaked snake	*Rhamphiophis oxyrhynchus rostratus*
Western stripe-bellied sand snake	*Psammophis subtaeniatus subtaeniatus*
Olive grass snake	*Psammophis phillipsii*
Angolan pygmy grass snake	*Psammophis angolensis*
Common purple-glossed snake	*Amblyodipsas polylepis polylepis*
Variable quill-snouted snake	*Xenocalamus bicolor bicolor*
Elongate quill-snouted snake	*Xenocalamus mechowii inornatus*
Bibron's stiletto snake	*Actraspis bibronii*
Angolan green snake	*Philothamnus angolensis*
Variegated bush snake	*Philothamnus semivariegatus semivariegatus*
Barotse water snake	*Crotaphopeltis barotseensis*
Eastern tiger snake	*Telescopus semiannulatus semiannulatus*
Boomslang	*Dispholidus typus typus*
Southern vine snake	*Thelotornis capensis capensis*
Oates' vine snake	*Thelotornis capensis oatesii*
African egg-eating snake	*Dasypeltis scabra*
Shield-nosed snake	*Aspidelaps scutatus scutatus*
Angolan cobra	*Naja haje anchietae*
Mozambique spitting cobra	*Naja mossambica*
Black mamba	*Dendroaspis polylepis*
Rhombic night adder	*Causus rhombeatus*
Puff adder	*Bitis arietans arietans*

Fish

ENGLISH	GENERIC	ENGLISH	GENERIC
Bulldog	*Marcusenius macrolepidotus*	Okavango catfish	*Clarias dumerilii*
Western bottlenose	*Mormyrus lacerda*	Sharptooth catfish	*Clarias gariepinus*
Churchill	*Petrocephalus catostoma*	Blunttooth catfish	*Clarias ngamensis*
Striped robber	*Alestes lateralis*	Spotted squeaker	*Synodontis nigromaculatus*
Tigerfish	*Hydrocynus vittatus*	Leopard squeaker	*Synodontis leopardinus*
Silver robber	*Micralestes acutidens*	Striped topminnow	*Aplocheilichthys katangae*
Okavango robber	*Rhabdalestes maunensis*	Barred jewelfish	*Hemichromis elongatus*
African pike	*Hepsetus odoe*	Threespot tilapia	*Oreochromis andersonii*
Multibar citharine	*Hemigrammocharax multifasciatus*	Greenhead tilapia	*Oreochromis macrochir*
		Southern mouthbrooder	*Pseudocrenilabris philander*
Broadbarred citharine	*Nannocharax macropterus*	Thinfaced largemouth	*Serranochromis angusticeps*
Hyphen barb	*Barbus bifrenatus*		
Spottail barb	*Barbus afrovernayi*	Nembwe	*Serranochromis robustus*
Beira barb	*Barbus radiatus*	Redbreasted tilapia	*Tilapia rendalli*
River sardine	*Mesobola brevianalis*	Banded tilapia	*Tilapia sparrmanii*
Zambezi grunter	*Auchenoglanis ngamensis*	Manyspined climbing perch	*Ctenopoma multispinis*
Silver catfish	*Schilbe mystus*	Longtailed spiny eel	*Afromastacembelus frenatus*

Birds

ENGLISH	NO.*	GENERIC NAME	ENGLISH	NO.	GENERIC NAME
Waterfowl			Purple gallinule	(223)	*Porphyrio porphyrio*
Dabchick	(8)	*Tachybaptus ruficollis*	Lesser gallinule	(224)	*Porphyrula alleni*
White pelican	(49)	*Pelecanus onocrotalus*	Moorhen	(226)	*Gallinula chloropus*
Pinkbacked pelican	(50)	*Pelecanus rufescens*	Lesser moorhen	(227)	*Gallinula angulata*
Whitebreasted cormorant	(55)	*Phalacrocorax carbo*			
Reed cormorant	(58)	*Phalacrocorax africanus*			
Darter	(60)	*Anhinga melanogaster*	**Kingfishers**		
Whitefaced duck	(99)	*Dendrocygna viduata*			
Fulvous duck	(100)	*Dendrocygna bicolor*	Pied kingfisher	(428)	*Ceryle rudis*
Whitebacked duck	(101)	*Thalassornis leuconotus*	Giant kingfisher	(429)	*Ceryle maxima*
Egyptian goose	(102)	*Alopochen aegyptiacus*	Halfcollared kingfisher	(430)	*Alcedo semitorquata*
Yellowbilled duck	(104)	*Anas undulata*	Malachite kingfisher	(431)	*Alcedo cristata*
Cape teal	(106)	*Anas capensis*	Pygmy kingfisher	(432)	*Ispidina picta*
Hottentot teal	(107)	*Anas hottentota*	Woodland kingfisher	(433)	*Halcyon senegalensis*
Redbilled teal	(108)	*Anas erythrorhyncha*	Brownhooded kingfisher	(435)	*Halcyon albiventris*
Southern pochard	(113)	*Netta erythrophthalma*	Greyhooded kingfisher	(436)	*Halcyon leucocephala*
Pygmy goose	(114)	*Nettapus auritus*	Striped kingfisher	(437)	*Halcyon chelicuti*
Knobbilled duck	(115)	*Sarkidiornis melanotos*			
Spurwinged goose	(116)	*Plectropterus gambensis*			
Redknobbed coot	(228)	*Fulica cristata*	**Waders**		
African finfoot	(229)	*Podica senegalensis*			
			Grey heron	(62)	*Ardea cinerea*
			Blackheaded heron	(63)	*Ardea melanocephala*
Birds of aquatic vegetation			Goliath heron	(64)	*Ardea goliath*
			Great white egret	(66)	*Egretta alba*
Lesser jacana	(241)	*Microparra capensis*	Little egret	(67)	*Egretta garzetta*
African jacana	(240)	*Actophilornis africanus*	Yellowbilled egret	(68)	*Egretta intermedia*
African rail	(210)	*Rallus caerulescens*	Black egret	(69)	*Egretta ardesiaca*
Corncrake	(211)	*Crex crex*	Slaty egret	(70)	*Egretta vinaceigula*
African crake	(212)	*Crex egregia*	Cattle egret	(71)	*Bubulcus ibis*
Black crake	(213)	*Amaurornis flavirostris*	Squacco heron	(72)	*Ardeola ralloides*
Spotted crake	(214)	*Porzana porzana*	Greenbacked heron	(74)	*Butorides striatus*
Baillon's crake	(215)	*Porzana pusilla*	Rufousbellied heron	(75)	*Butorides rufiventris*
Striped crake	(216)	*Aenigmatolimnas marginalis*	Blackcrowned night heron	(76)	*Nycticorax nycticorax*

ENGLISH	NO.	GENERIC NAME	ENGLISH	NO.	GENERIC NAME
Whitebacked night heron	(77)	*Gorsachius leuconotus*	Crowned plover	(255)	*Vanellus coronatus*
Little bittern	(78)	*Ixobrychus minutus*	Blacksmith plover	(258)	*Vanellus armatus*
Dwarf bittern	(79)	*Ixobrychus sturmii*	Whitecrowned plover	(259)	*Vanellus albiceps*
Bittern	(80)	*Botaurus stellaris*	Wattled plover	(260)	*Vanellus senegallus*
Hamerkop	(81)	*Scopus umbretta*	Longtoed plover	(261)	*Vanellus crassirostris*
White stork	(83)	*Ciconia ciconia*	Common sandpiper	(264)	*Tringa hypoleucos*
Black stork	(84)	*Ciconia nigra*	Green sandpiper	(265)	*Tringa ochropus*
Abdim's stork	(85)	*Ciconia abdimii*	Wood sandpiper	(266)	*Tringa glareola*
Woollynecked stork	(86)	*Ciconia episcopus*	Marsh sandpiper	(269)	*Tringa stagnatilis*
Openbilled stork	(87)	*Anastomus lamelligerus*	Greenshank	(270)	*Tringa nebularia*
Saddlebilled stork	(88)	*Ephippiorhynchus senegalensis*	Curlew sandpiper	(272)	*Calidris ferruginea*
			Little stint	(274)	*Calidris minuta*
Marabou stork	(89)	*Leptoptilos crumeniferus*	Ruff	(284)	*Philomachus pugnax*
Yellowbilled stork	(90)	*Mycteria ibis*	Ethiopian snipe	(286)	*Gallinago nigripennis*
Sacred ibis	(91)	*Threskiornis aethiopicus*	Painted snipe	(242)	*Rostratula benghalensis*
Glossy ibis	(93)	*Plegadis falcinellus*	Avocet	(294)	*Recurvirostra avosetta*
Hadeda ibis	(94)	*Bostrychia hagedash*	Blackwinged stilt	(295)	*Himantopus himantopus*
African spoonbill	(95)	*Platalea alba*	Spotted dikkop	(297)	*Burhinus capensis*
African skimmer	(343)	*Rynchops flavirostris*	Water dikkop	(298)	*Burhinus vermiculatus*
			Temminck's courser	(300)	*Cursorius temminckii*
			Bronzewinged courser	(303)	*Rhinoptilus chalcopterus*
			Redwinged pratincole	(304)	*Glareola pratincola*
			Blackwinged pratincole	(305)	*Glareola nordmanni*

Bee-eaters, rollers

ENGLISH	NO.	GENERIC NAME
European bee-eater	(438)	*Merops apiaster*
Bluecheeked bee-eater	(440)	*Merops persicus*
Carmine bee-eater	(441)	*Merops nubicoides*
Whitefronted bee-eater	(443)	*Merops bullockoides*
Little bee-eater	(444)	*Merops pusillus*
Swallowtailed bee-eater	(445)	*Merops hirundineus*
European roller	(446)	*Coracias garrulus*
Lilacbreasted roller	(447)	*Coracias caudata*
Purple roller	(449)	*Coracias naevia*
Broadbilled roller	(450)	*Eurystomus glaucurus*

Birds of prey

ENGLISH	NO.	GENERIC NAME
Secretarybird	(118)	*Sagittarius serpentarius*
Yellowbilled kite	(126)	*Milvus migrans parasitus*
Blackshouldered kite	(127)	*Elanus caeruleus*
Bat hawk	(129)	*Macheiramphus alcinus*
Tawny eagle	(132)	*Aquila rapax*
Steppe eagle	(133)	*Aquila nipalensis*
Lesser spotted eagle	(134)	*Aquila pomarina*
Wahlberg's eagle	(135)	*Aquila wahlbergi*
Booted eagle	(136)	*Hieraaetus pennatus*
African hawk eagle	(137)	*Hieraaetus fasciatus*
Longcrested eagle	(139)	*Lophaetus occipitalis*
Martial eagle	(140)	*Polemaetus bellicosus*

Floodplain/Grassland birds

ENGLISH	NO.	GENERIC NAME
Wattled crane	(207)	*Grus carunculata*
Ringed plover	(245)	*Charadrius hiaticula*
Whitefronted plover	(246)	*Charadrius marginatus*
Kittlitz's plover	(248)	*Charadrius pecuarius*
Threebanded plover	(249)	*Charadrius tricollaris*
Caspian plover	(252)	*Charadrius asiaticus*

*Numbers as in Roberts *Birds of South Africa*.

ENGLISH	NO.	GENERIC NAME
Brown snake eagle	(142)	*Circaetus cinereus*
Blackbreasted snake eagle	(143)	*Circaetus gallicus*
Western banded snake eagle	(145)	*Circaetus cinerascens*
Bateleur	(146)	*Terathopius ecaudatus*
African fish eagle	(148)	*Haliaeetus vocifer*
Steppe buzzard	(149)	*Buteo buteo vulpinus*
Lizard buzzard	(154)	*Kaupifalco monogrammicus*
Ovambo sparrowhawk	(156)	*Accipiter ovampensis*
Little sparrowhawk	(157)	*Accipiter minullus*
Little banded goshawk	(159)	*Accipiter badius*
African goshawk	(160)	*Accipiter tachiro*
Gabar goshawk	(161)	*Micronisus gabar*
Dark chanting goshawk	(163)	*Melierax metabates*
African marsh harrier	(165)	*Circus ranivorus*
Montagu's harrier	(166)	*Circus pygargus*
Pallid harrier	(167)	*Circus macrourus*
Gymnogene	(169)	*Polyboroides typus*
Peregrine falcon	(171)	*Falco peregrinus*
Lanner falcon	(172)	*Falco biarmicus*
Hobby falcon	(173)	*Falco subbuteo*
African hobby falcon	(174)	*Falco cuvierii*
Rednecked falcon	(178)	*Falco chicquera*
Western redfooted kestrel	(179)	*Falco vespertinus*
Greater kestrel	(182)	*Falco rupicoloides*
Lesser kestrel	(183)	*Falco naumanni*
Dickinson's kestrel	(185)	*Falco dickinsoni*

Game birds — largely terrestrial

ENGLISH	NO.	GENERIC NAME
Coqui francolin	(188)	*Francolinus coqui*
Crested francolin	(189)	*Francolinus sephaena*

ENGLISH	NO.	GENERIC NAME
Redbilled francolin	(194)	*Francolinus adspersus*
Swainson's francolin	(199)	*Francolinus swainsonii*
Harlequin quail	(201)	*Coturnix delegorguei*
Helmeted guineafowl	(203)	*Numida meleagris*
Kurrichane buttonquail	(205)	*Turnix sylvatica*

Nocturnal birds

ENGLISH	NO.	GENERIC NAME
Barn owl	(392)	*Tyto alba*
Wood owl	(394)	*Strix woodfordii*
Marsh owl	(395)	*Asio capensis*
Scops owl	(396)	*Otus senegalensis*
Whitefaced owl	(397)	*Otus leucotis*
Pearlspotted owl	(398)	*Glaucidium perlatum*
Spotted eagle owl	(401)	*Bubo africanus*
Giant eagle owl	(402)	*Bubo lacteus*
Pel's fishing owl	(403)	*Scotopelia peli*

ENGLISH	NO.	GENERIC NAME
Fierynecked nightjar	(405)	*Caprimulgus pectoralis*
Rufoускheeked nightjar	(406)	*Caprimulgus rufigena*
Freckled nightjar	(408)	*Caprimulgus tristigma*
Mozambique nightjar	(409)	*Caprimulgus fossii*
Pennantwinged nightjar	(410)	*Macrodipteryx vexillaria*

Woodland and savannah birds

ENGLISH	NO.	GENERIC NAME
Ostrich	(1)	*Struthio camelus*
Namaqua sandgrouse	(344)	*Pterocles namaqua*
Burchell's sandgrouse	(345)	*Pterocles burchelli*
Yellowthroated sandgrouse	(346)	*Pterocles gutturalis*
Doublebanded sandgrouse	(347)	*Pterocles bicinctus*
Redeyed dove	(352)	*Streptopelia semitorquata*
Mourning dove	(353)	*Streptopelia decipiens*
Cape turtle dove	(354)	*Streptopelia capicola*
Laughing dove	(355)	*Streptopelia senegalensis*
Namaqua dove	(356)	*Oena capensis*
Greenspotted dove	(358)	*Turtur chalcospilos*
Green pigeon	(361)	*Treron calva*
Meyer's parrot	(364)	*Poicephalus meyeri*
Grey lourie	(373)	*Corythaixoides concolor*
African cuckoo	(375)	*Cuculus gularis*
Redchested cuckoo	(377)	*Cuculus solitarius*
Black cuckoo	(378)	*Cuculus clamosus*
Great spotted cuckoo	(380)	*Clamator glandarius*
Striped cuckoo	(381)	*Clamator levaillantii*
Jacobin cuckoo	(382)	*Clamator jacobinus*
Klaas's cuckoo	(385)	*Chrysococcyx klaas*
Diederik cuckoo	(386)	*Chrysococcyx caprius*
Copperytailed coucal	(389)	*Centropus cupreicaudus*
Senegal coucal	(390)	*Centropus senegalensis*
Hoopoe	(451)	*Upupa epops*
Redbilled woodhoopoe	(452)	*Phoeniculus purpureus*
Scimitarbilled woodhoopoe	(454)	*Phoeniculus cyanomelas*
Grey hornbill	(457)	*Tockus nasutus*
Redbilled hornbill	(458)	*Tockus erythrorhynchus*
Yellowbilled hornbill	(459)	*Tockus flavirostris*
Crowned hornbill	(460)	*Tockus alboterminatus*
Bradfield's hornbill	(461)	*Tockus bradfieldi*
Ground hornbill	(463)	*Bucorvus leadbeateri*
Blackcollared barbet	(464)	*Lybius torquatus*
Pied barbet	(465)	*Lybius leucomelas*
Crested barbet	(473)	*Trachyphonus vaillantii*
Greater honeyguide	(474)	*Indicator indicator*
Lesser honeyguide	(476)	*Indicator minor*
Sharpbilled honeyguide	(478)	*Prodotiscus regulus*
Bennett's woodpecker	(481)	*Campethera bennettii*
Goldentailed woodpecker	(483)	*Campethera abingoni*
Cardinal woodpecker	(486)	*Dendropicos fuscescens*
Bearded woodpecker	(487)	*Thripias namaquus*
Monotonous lark	(493)	*Mirafra passerina*
Rufousnaped lark	(494)	*Mirafra africana*
Flappet lark	(496)	*Mirafra rufocinnamomea*
Fawncoloured lark	(497)	*Mirafra africanoides*
Sabota lark	(498)	*Mirafra sabota*
Dusky lark	(505)	*Pinarocorys nigricans*

ENGLISH	NO.	GENERIC NAME
Redcapped lark	(507)	*Calandrella cinerea*
Chestnutbacked finchlark	(515)	*Eremopterix leucotis*
Black cuckooshrike	(538)	*Campephaga flava*
Whitebreasted cuckooshrike	(539)	*Coracina pectoralis*
Forktailed drongo	(541)	*Dicrurus adsimilis*
European golden oriole	(543)	*Oriolus oriolus*
African golden oriole	(544)	*Oriolus auratus*
Blackheaded oriole	(545)	*Oriolus larvatus*
Ashy grey tit	(552)	*Parus cinerascens*
Southern black tit	(554)	*Parus niger*
Cape penduline tit	(557)	*Anthoscopus minutus*
Grey penduline tit	(558)	*Anthoscopus caroli*
Arrowmarked babbler	(560)	*Turdoides jardineii*
Blackfaced babbler	(561)	*Turdoides melanops*
Whiterumped babbler	(562)	*Turdoides leucopygius*
Pied babbler	(563)	*Turdoides bicolor*
Blackeyed bulbul	(568)	*Pycnonotus barbatus*
Terrestrial bulbul	(569)	*Phyllastrephus terrestris*
Kurrichane thrush	(576)	*Turdus libonyana*
Groundscraper thrush	(580)	*Turdus litsitsirupa*
Capped wheatear	(587)	*Oenanthe pileata*
Arnot's chat	(594)	*Thamnolaea arnoti*
Anteating chat	(595)	*Myrmecocichla formicivora*
Stonechat	(596)	*Saxicola torquata*
Heuglin's robin	(599)	*Cossypha heuglini*
Whitebrowed robin	(613)	*Erythropygia leucophrys*
Garden warbler	(619)	*Sylvia borin*
Whitethroat	(620)	*Sylvia communis*
Titbabbler	(621)	*Parisoma subcaeruleum*
Icterine warbler	(625)	*Hippolais icterina*
Great reed warbler	(628)	*Acrocephalus arundinaceus*
African marsh warbler	(631)	*Acrocephalus baeticatus*
European sedge warbler	(634)	*Acrocephalus schoenobaenus*
Cape reed warbler	(635)	*Acrocephalus gracilirostris*
Greater swamp warbler	(636)	*Acrocephalus rufescens*
African sedge warbler	(638)	*Bradypterus baboecala*
Willow warbler	(643)	*Phylloscopus trochilus*
Yellowbreasted apalis	(648)	*Apalis flavida*
Longbilled crombec	(651)	*Sylvietta rufescens*
Yellowbellied eremomela	(653)	*Eremomela icteropygialis*

ENGLISH	NO.	GENERIC NAME	ENGLISH	NO.	GENERIC NAME
Greencapped eremomela	(655)	*Eremomela scotops*	Greater blue-eared starling	(765)	*Lamprotornis chalybaeus*
Burntnecked eremomela	(656)	*Eremomela usticollis*	Yellowbilled oxpecker	(771)	*Buphagus africanus*
Bleating warbler	(657)	*Camaroptera brachyura*	Redbilled oxpecker	(772)	*Buphagus erythrorhynchus*
Barred warbler	(658)	*Camaroptera fasciolata*			
Fantailed cisticola	(664)	*Cisticola juncidis*	Marico sunbird	(779)	*Nectarinia mariquensis*
Desert cisticola	(665)	*Cisticola aridula*	Whitebellied sunbird	(787)	*Nectarinia talatala*
Tinkling cisticola	(671)	*Cisticola rufilata*	Scarletchested sunbird	(791)	*Nectarinia senegalensis*
Blackbacked cisticola	(675)	*Cisticola galactotes*	Black sunbird	(792)	*Nectarinia amethystina*
Chirping cisticola	(676)	*Cisticola pipiens*	Collared sunbird	(793)	*Anthreptes collaris*
Neddicky	(681)	*Cisticola fulvicapilla*	Yellow white-eye	(797)	*Zosterops senegalensis*
Blackchested prinia	(685)	*Prinia flavicans*	Redbilled buffalo weaver	(798)	*Bubalornis niger*
Spotted flycatcher	(689)	*Muscicapa striata*	Whitebrowed sparrowweaver	(799)	*Plocepasser mahali*
Bluegrey flycatcher	(691)	*Muscicapa caerulescens*	Greyheaded sparrow	(804)	*Passer griseus*
Fantailed flycatcher	(693)	*Myioparus plumbeus*	Yellowthroated sparrow	(805)	*Petronia superciliaris*
Black flycatcher	(694)	*Melaenornis pammelaina*	Scalyfeathered finch	(806)	*Sporopipes squamifrons*
Marico flycatcher	(695)	*Melaenornis mariquensis*	Thickbilled weaver	(807)	*Amblyospiza albifrons*
Pallid flycatcher	(696)	*Melaenornis pallidus*	Spectacled weaver	(810)	*Ploceus ocularis*
Chinspot batis	(701)	*Batis molitor*	Spottedbacked weaver	(811)	*Ploceus cucullatus*
Paradise flycatcher	(710)	*Terpsiphone viridis*	Masked weaver	(814)	*Ploceus velatus*
African pied wagtail	(711)	*Motacilla aguimp*	Lesser masked weaver	(815)	*Ploceus intermedius*
Cape wagtail	(713)	*Motacilla capensis*	Golden weaver	(816)	*Ploceus xanthops*
Yellow wagtail	(714)	*Motacilla flava*	Brownthroated weaver	(818)	*Ploceus xanthopterus*
Richard's pipit	(716)	*Anthus novaeseelandiae*	Redheaded weaver	(819)	*Anaplectes rubriceps*
Longbilled pipit	(717)	*Anthus similis*	Redbilled quelea	(821)	*Quelea quelea*
Plainbacked pipit	(718)	*Anthus leucophrys*	Red bishop	(824)	*Euplectes orix*
Buffy pipit	(719)	*Anthus vaalensis*	Redshouldered widow	(828)	*Euplectes axillaris*
Pinkthroated longclaw	(730)	*Macronyx ameliae*	Whitewinged widow	(829)	*Euplectes albonotatus*
Lesser grey shrike	(713)	*Lanius minor*	Melba finch	(834)	*Pytilia melba*
Fiscal shrike	(732)	*Lanius collaris*	Jameson's firefinch	(841)	*Lagonosticta rhodopareia*
Redbacked shrike	(733)	*Lanius collurio*			
Longtailed shrike	(735)	*Corvinella melanoleuca*	Redbilled firefinch	(842)	*Lagonosticta senegala*
Swamp boubou	(738)	*Laniarius bicolor*	Brown firefinch	(843)	*Lagonosticta nitidula*
Crimsonbreasted shrike	(739)	*Laniarius atrococcineus*	Blue waxbill	(844)	*Uraeginthus angolensis*
Puffback	(740)	*Dryoscopus cubla*	Violeteared waxbill	(845)	*Uraeginthus granatinus*
Brubru	(741)	*Nilaus afer*	Common waxbill	(846)	*Estrilda astrild*
Threestreaked tchagra	(743)	*Tchagra australis*	Blackcheeked waxbill	(847)	*Estrilda erythronotos*
Blackcrowned tchagra	(744)	*Tchagra senegala*	Quail finch	(852)	*Ortygospiza atricollis*
Orangebreasted bush shrike	(748)	*Telophorus sulfureopectus*	Orangebreasted waxbill	(854)	*Sporaeginthus subflavus*
White helmetshrike	(753)	*Prionops plumatus*	Cutthroat finch	(855)	*Amadina fasciata*
Redbilled helmetshrike	(754)	*Prionops retzii*	Shafttailed whydah	(861)	*Vidua regia*
Whitecrowned shrike	(756)	*Eurocephalus anguitimens*	Paradise whydah	(862)	*Vidua paradisea*
			Black widowfinch	(864)	*Vidua funerea*
Wattled starling	(760)	*Creatophora cinerea*	Purple widowfinch	(865)	*Vidua purpurascens*
Plumcoloured starling	(761)	*Cinnyricinclus leucogaster*	Steelblue widowfinch	(867)	*Vidua chalybeata*
			Yelloweyed canary	(869)	*Serinus mozambicus*
Burchell's starling	(762)	*Lamprotornis australis*	Blackthroated canary	(870)	*Serinus atrogularis*
Longtailed starling	(763)	*Lamprotornis mevesii*	Goldenbreasted bunting	(884)	*Emberiza flaviventris*
Glossy starling	(764)	*Lamprotornis nitens*			

Bibliography

Anderson, A.J. 1976: Weather of the Okavango Delta. In *Symposium on the Okavango Delta*. 1976. The Botswana Society, Gaborone.

Andersson, C.J. 1856: *Lake Ngami; or explorations and discoveries during four years wandering in the wilds of south western Africa*. Facsimile Edition 1967, C. Struik, Cape Town.

Astle, W.L., and Graham, A. 1976: Ecological investigations of the UNDP in the Okavango Delta. In *Symposium on the Okavango Delta*. 1976. The Botswana Society, Gaborone.

Auerbach, R.D. 1987: *The Reptiles and Amphibians of Botswana*. Mokwepa Consultants, Gaborone.

Biggs, R.C. 1976: The effects of the seasonal flood regime on the ecology of Chief's Island and the adjacent floodplain system. In *Symposium on the Okavango Delta*. 1976. The Botswana Society, Gaborone.

Brown, L. 1980: *The African Fish Eagle*. Purnell and Sons, Cape Town.

Carruthers, V. 1976: *A Guide to the Identification of the Frogs of the Witwatersrand*. Conservation Press, Johannesburg.

Child, G. and Robbel, H. 1975: Drowning of lechwe by spotted hyaena. *Mammalia* 39:4.

Cooke, H.J. 1976: The Palaeogeography of the middle Kalahari of Northern Botswana and adjacent areas. In *Symposium on the Okavango Delta*. 1976. The Botswana Society, Gaborone.

Cooke, H.J. 1984: Landform evolution in the context of climatic change and neo-tectonism in the middle Kalahari of north central Botswana. *Transactions of the Institute of British Geography:* N.S. 5: 80—99.

Denny, P. (Ed), 1985: *The Ecology and Management of African Wetland Vegetation*. Dr W. Junk, Dordrecht, The Netherlands.

Games, I. 1983: Observations on the Sitatunga *Tragelaphus spekei selousi* in the Okavango Delta of Botswana. *Biological Conservation* 27. 157—170.

Gibbs-Russell, G.E. 1977: Key to vascular aquatic plants in Rhodesia. *Kirkia* vol 10, 2.

Greenwood, P.G. and Carruthers, R.M. 1973: Geophysical Surveys in the Okavango Delta, Botswana. *Institute of Geological Sciences,* Applied Geophysics Unit. Report No. 15.

Grove, A.T. 1969: Landforms and climatic change in the Kalahari and Ngamiland. *Geographical Journal* 135, 2:191—212.

Hutchins, D.G. *et al.* 1976: A summary of the geology, seismicity, geomorphology and hydrogeology of the Okavango Delta. *Bulletin of the Geological Survey of Botswana* 7.

Maclean, G.L. 1985: *Roberts' Birds of Southern Africa*. The John Voelcker Book Fund, Cape Town.

Marais, E. 1937. *The Soul of the White Ant*. Translation by W. de Kok. Published by Penguin Books, U.K. 1973.

McCarthy, J., *et al:* The roles of sedimentation and plant growth in changing flow patterns in the Okavango, Botswana. *South African Journal of Science,* 83 pp 579—584.

Merron, G.S. 1987: Predator-Prey interactions in the Okavango Delta: The annual catfish run, October-December, 1986. *Investigational Report* No 25, J.L.B. Smith Institute of Ichthyology.

Minshull, J.L. 1985: A collection of fish from the Lower Okavango Swamp, Botswana, with comments on aspects of their ecology. *Arnoldia Zimbabwe* 9(20): 277—290.

Patterson, L. 1976: An Introduction to the Ecology and Zoo-geography of the Okavango Delta. In *Symposium on the Okavango Delta*. 1976. The Botswana Society, Gaborone.

Robbel, H. and Child, G. 1976: *Notes on the Ecology of the Moremi Wildlife Reserve*. Dept. of Wildlife and National Parks, Govt. Botswana.

Scholtz, C.H. 1975: Seismicity, Tectonics and Seismic Hazard of the Okavango Delta, Botswana. *Final report to UNDP on the Okavango Delta*. Geological Survey, Botswana.

Scholz, C.H. *et al.* 1976: Evidence for Incipient Rifting in Southern Africa. *Geophysical Journal of the Royal Astronomical Society* 44 pp 135—144.

Scholz, C.H. and Holm, E. (Eds) 1985: *Insects of Southern Africa*. Butterworth Publishers, Durban.

Shaw, P.A. 1985: The desiccation of Lake Ngami: a historical perspective. *The Geographical Journal* 51:3.

Skelton, P.H., *et al.* 1985: The fishes of the Okavango Drainage System in Angola, South West Africa and Botswana: Taxonomy and Distribution. *Ichthyological Bulletin of the J.L.B. Smith Institute of Ichthyology* No 50.

Smith, P.A. 1976: An outline of the Vegetation of the Okavango drainage system. In *Symposium on the Okavango Delta*, Botswana Society, Gaborone.

Smithers, R.N. 1971: The Mammals of Botswana. *Museum Memoir* No. 4. The Trustees of the National Museums of Rhodesia. Harare.

Smithers, R.N. 1983: *The Mammals of the Southern African Subregion*. University of Pretoria, Pretoria.

Thompson, K. 1976: The primary productivity of African wetlands with particular reference to the Okavango Delta. In *Symposium on the Okavango Delta*. 1976. The Botswana Society, Gaborone.

Tinley, K.L. 1966: *An Ecological Reconnaissance of the Moremi Wildlife Reserve*. Okavango Wildlife Society, Johannesburg.

Tlou, T. 1985: *A History of Ngamiland — 1750 to 1906 — the formation of an African state*. Macmillan, Botswana.

Wild, H. 1961: Harmful aquatic plants in Africa and Madagascar. Joint CCTA/CSA Project No. 14. *Kirkia* vol. 2.

Wilson, B.H. 1983: Some natural and man-made changes in the channels of the Okavango Delta. *Botswana Notes and Records* 15: pp 138.

Wilson, B.H., and Dincer, T. 1976: An introduction to the hydrology and hydrography of the Okavango Delta. In *Symposium on the Okavango Delta*. 1976. The Botswana Society, Gaborone.

Acknowledgements

This book is the result not only of the industry of the authors, but also of the help, advice and patience of a host of others. We wish to express our appreciation to everyone involved in any way; in particular, thanks are due to the following people:

The Government of Botswana and The Department of Wildlife and National Parks, for permission to undertake the work;

The staff of Okavango Tours and Safaris and Maun Office Services;

Lesajwa, local expert, guide and dice-man; Batselelweng Senkapau, sage;

Reiner and Birgit Köhler, Lance Cherry, Maureen Blogg, Hugh Patterson, Wendy Miller, Peter Sandenbergh, Russell Knight, John Bulger, Julia Cairns, Sally Barrow, Map Ives, Mike Watson, Teddy Egner — friends, neighbours and pillars of sanity;

Paul Sheller, Janette Pedersen, Tony and Yoey Graham, for hospitality and first aid;

Bill Hamilton and Glenn Merron for biological advice;

John Loveridge for help with reptiles and amphibians;

Pete Smith for a botanical perusal of the text;

Katherine Verbeek, Nirmala Rao-Adapa, Mattias Nilsson, Ann Gollifer, Frances Coombs, for patience in the face of extraordinary chaos in their homes and lives;

Hugh Murray-Hudson, for contributing to the text;

Perdi Perdicopanis and Glenn Wakfer.

Kind permission to use illustrations: Carta Press (1969), Harper and Bros (1858), Lloyd and Co (1855), Routledge (1874), Barnes & Co (1887), Frederick Warne and Co. (1893/4).

The baboon photographs on pages 112-113 are reproduced by courtesy of John Bulger. Satellite photos of the earth and the Okavango are reproduced by courtesy of the CSIR.

Fish eagles flying. Your minimum camera speed should be 1/500 second. Dawn and sunset with side light are best to avoid shadow under the eagle. Fish eagles will take fish fed to them.

Aerial photos. Your minimum camera speed should be 1/250 second. Use a plane with the door or window removed, or climb a tree for a different perspective.

Scenic photos. The best time for scenic shots is around dawn and sunset when the light is soft. Midday light is harsh.

Underwater photos. An underwater camera or housing and wide angle lenses work best as you can get closer to the subject, which avoids murkiness and gives better colour.

Animal photos. A mokoro makes an excellent platform for photographing animals. Keep quiet and don't make any sudden movements. No hides were used for the photos in this book.